INFORMATION TECHNOLOGY LAW

CONSUMER PROTECTION ONLINE

MICHAEL E. DETURBIDE

GENERAL EDITOR: SUNNY HANDA

LexisNexis®
Butterworths

Consumer Protection Online
© LexisNexis Canada Inc. 2006
October 2006

Members of the LexisNexis Group worldwide

Canada	LexisNexis Canada Inc, 123 Commerce Valley Drive East, Suite 700, MARKHAM, Ontario
Argentina	Abeledo Perrot, Jurisprudencia Argentina and Depalma, BUENOS AIRES
Australia	Butterworths, a Division of Reed International Books Australia Pty Ltd, CHATSWOOD, New South Wales
Austria	ARD Betriebsdienst and Verlag Orac, VIENNA
Chile	Publitecsa and Conosur Ltda, SANTIAGO DE CHILE
Czech Republic	Orac sro, PRAGUE
France	Éditions du Juris-Classeur SA, PARIS
Hong Kong	Butterworths Asia (Hong Kong), HONG KONG
Hungary	Hvg Orac, BUDAPEST
India	Butterworths India, NEW DELHI
Ireland	Butterworths (Ireland) Ltd, DUBLIN
Italy	Giuffré, MILAN
Malaysia	Malayan Law Journal Sdn Bhd, KUALA LUMPUR
New Zealand	Butterworths of New Zealand, WELLINGTON
Poland	Wydawnictwa Prawnicze PWN, WARSAW
Singapore	Butterworths Asia, SINGAPORE
South Africa	Butterworth Publishers (Pty) Ltd, DURBAN
Switzerland	Stämpfli Verlag AG, BERNE
United Kingdom	Butterworths Tolley, a Division of Reed Elsevier (UK), LONDON, WC2A
USA	LexisNexis, DAYTON, Ohio

Library and Archives Canada Cataloguing in Publication

Deturbide, Michael E. (Michael Eugene), 1957-
    Consumer protection online / Michael Deturbide.

(Information technology law series)
Includes index.
ISBN 0-433-45106-8

        1. Consumer protection—Law and legislation—Canada.
2. Electronic commerce—Law and legislation—Canada.
I. Title. II. Series.

KE1599.D48 2006   343.7107'1   C2006-904866-5
KF1609.D48 2006

Printed and bound in Canada.

ABOUT THE AUTHOR

Michael E. Deturbide, B.Sc., B.J., LL.B., LL.M., is an Associate Professor of Law at Dalhousie Law School, Halifax. He is also Technology Counsel to the Atlantic Canada law firm, McInnes Cooper. Professor Deturbide is a founder of the Law and Technology Institute at Dalhousie (<http://lati.law.dal.ca>), co-editor-in-chief of the Canadian Journal of Law and Technology (<http://cjlt.dal.ca>), and co-author, with Teresa Scassa, of the text *Electronic Commerce and Internet Law in Canada*. He has written and lectured on information technology law issues in North America, Europe, and Australia.

ABOUT THE GENERAL EDITOR

Dr. Sunny Handa is a partner with the international law firm of Blake, Cassels & Graydon LLP and is co-head of the firm's national Information Technology Group. Dr. Handa deals with information technology, intellectual property, e-commerce and communication law matters, and is also Professor of Law (adj.) at McGill University where he teaches in the areas of high technology and intellectual property law. He is the author of *Copyright Law in Canada* and a co-author of *Communications Law in Canada* and *E-Commerce Legislation and Materials in Canada*, all published by LexisNexis Canada, as well as numerous other publications. Dr. Handa also is the creator/developer and General Editor of the Information Technology Law book series and in this role develops, structures and edits each title.

ABOUT THE SERIES

Information Technology Law is an exciting new series of books designed to assist lawyers and business professionals in demystifying complex information technology law issues while requiring no specific prior knowledge on the part of the reader. Each book will focus on a particular cutting edge information technology law subject. The creator and general editor of the series is Dr. Sunny Handa. Each book will be written by different leading Canadian IT jurists with expertise in the particular area. Upcoming titles will cover topics including web agreements and policies, IT outsourcing, open source software, and e-mail. Other titles will continue to be added to the series in coming years.

FOREWORD

The area of consumer protection in the online world is a thorny one and, given the rapid pace with which online global electronic consumerism has grown, the issue has taken on great significance. Consumers purchasing goods and services online often naively assume, because the phenomenon of electronic consumerism has grown to be so large and receives so much press, that the law has kept up and that they continue to enjoy the same rights and access to a justice system to enforce those rights as they would in the bricks and mortar world. Yet, those who practise law in the area know this to be woefully untrue.

The application of consumer protection laws and commercial law to the online environment is fraught with a number of key obstacles. For example, online retailing often takes place across provincial and even national borders. This is quite different from the typical shopping experience that most consumers are used to, whereby they walk to their corner store and buy their product or where they call a plumber or an electrician who shows up at their house to perform the necessary maintenance. In an online environment, these very same consumers are purchasing goods and services across borders and often have very little chance of enforcing contractual obligations should anything go wrong. Further, it is even often unknown to the consumer which laws will in fact apply. These are only a few examples of some of the issues that are addressed in this, the fourth volume, of the IT Law Series.

Law professor Michael Deturbide has a good deal of experience in consumer protection and commercial law and he is also a well respected IT jurist. He has drawn on his expertise to write a very accessible text that highlights the extreme complexity of the consumer protection area. All of us, as consumers, as well as those who offer their goods or services online, would benefit from reading this book. Combined with the Web law book (the last book in the IT Law Series), these two provide a comprehensive approach to doing business online.

This book also offers you a snapshot of the plethora of laws that apply, both federally and provincially, in Canada to doing business as an online consumer. Michael has also provided excerpts from relevant legislation as well as a table of concordance to help navigate through this maze of laws.

I know that after reading this text, you will find that this altogether difficult and complex area of law will be much easier to navigate. I congratulate Michael on this wonderful work.

Sunny Handa, Editor
July 31, 2006

ACKNOWLEDGMENTS

One of the many benefits of working in a thriving academic environment such as the Law and Technology Institute at Dalhousie Law School is the availability of talented law students to assist with research projects. I want to express my thanks to student assistant Travis Johnson, particularly for his comprehensive research skills in assembling the concordance in Chapter 2. I also wish to thank Carolle Crooks, a former student who has gone on to great achievements in law and dance, for her thorough investigation of spyware and identity theft issues. Thanks also to Lynda Corkum, who provided superlative secretarial assistance, to Sunny Handa for his editorial comments and original idea for this series, and to Danann Hawes for shepherding the book to publication.

Finally, thanks to Joanne for her constant support throughout.

TABLE OF CONTENTS

Page

About the Author iii
About the General Editor v
About the Series vii
Foreword ix
Acknowledgments xi
Table of Cases xv
Introduction xvii

CHAPTER 1 — THE ELECTRONIC CONTRACT 1

I. Formation of Online Contracts 1
   A. Offer and Invitation to Treat 3
   B. Acceptance 3
II. Notice of Terms 5
   A. Click-Wrap Agreements 5
   B. Browse-Wrap Agreements 8
Appendix I — Uniform Electronic Commerce Act 9

CHAPTER 2 — ONLINE CONSUMER PROTECTION LEGISLATION 19

I. History of Online Consumer Protection in Canada 20
II. The Internet Sales Contract Harmonization Template 22
   A. Application of the *Template* 23
   B. Disclosure of Information 23
   C. Contract Formation 25
   D. Cancellation 26
   E. Reversal of Credit Card Charges 28
III. Jurisdiction 29
IV. The *Competition Act* 32
Appendix I — Internet Sales Contract Harmonization Template 37
Appendix II — *Internet Sales Contract Harmonization Template*
   Concordance with Provincial Legislation 45

CHAPTER 3 — SECURITY OF PERSONAL INFORMATION 125

I. Legislative and Common Law Protection of Personal
   Information 126
   A. Criminal Laws Applicable to Identity Theft 126
   B. Privacy Legislation 129

      C.   Consumer Reporting Legislation 130

      D.   Legislative Reform 131

      E.   Common Law Liability 133

      F.   Legal Implications of Privacy and Security "Seals" 134

II.   "Phishing" 141

      A.   Existing Legislation Applicable to Phishing 143

          1.   *PIPEDA* 143

          2.   *Competition Act* 144

          3.   *Criminal Code* 144

      B.   Legislative Reform 146

III.   Identity Theft Education and Prevention Efforts 148

CHAPTER 4 — SPYWARE AND MALWARE 149

I.   Introduction 149

II.   Application of the *Criminal Code* to Malware and Spyware 151

      A.   Section 342.1: Unauthorized Use of a Computer 151

      B.   Section 430(1.1): Mischief in Relation to Data 154

      C.   Application of the *Criminal Code* Generally 155

III.   Application of *PIPEDA* to Spyware 155

IV.   Application of the *Competition Act* to Spyware 157

V.   Legislative Reform 158

VI.   Using the Common Law to Battle Spyware and Malware 161

      A.   Trespass to Chattels 161

      B.   Tort of Invasion of Privacy 164

VII. Consumer Awareness 165

Index 167

TABLE OF CASES

A

America Online, Inc. v. IMS, 24 F. Supp. 2d 548 (E.D. Va. 1998) 162

America Online, Inc. v. LCGM, Inc., 46 F. Supp. 2d 444 (E.D. Va. 1998) 162

America Online, Inc. v. Mendoza, 90 Cal. App. 4th 1 (2001) 6

Aspencer1.com v. Paysystems Corp., [2005] J.Q. No. 1573 (C.Q. Civ.) ... 2

C

Comb v. PayPal, Inc., 218 F. Supp. 2d 1165 (N.D. Cal. 2002) 7

Compuserve Inc. v. Cyber Promotions, 962 F. Supp. 1015, 1997 U.S. Dist. LEXIS 1997, 25 Media L. Rep 1545 (S.D. Ohio 1997) 161

Cooper v. Hobart, [2001] S.C.J. No. 76, 206 D.L.R. (4th) 193 ... 134

E

eBay, Inc. v. Bidder's Edge, Inc., 100 F. Supp. 2d 1058 (N.D. Cal. 2000) 162

F

Ferguson v. Friendfinders, Inc., 94 Cal.App. 4th 1255, 1267 [115 Cal. Rptr. 2d 258] (2002) 161

FTC v. Toysmart.com, LLC, 2000 U.S. Dist. LEXIS 21963 (D. Mass. 2000) 136

H

Hercules Managements Ltd. v. Ernst & Young, [1997] S.C.J. No. 51, [1997] 2 S.C.R. 165 ....138, 140

Hotmail Corp. v. Van$ Money Pie, Inc. 1998 WL 388389 (N.D. Cal., 1998, No. C 98-20064 JW) 162

Hubbert v. Dell Corp., 2005 WL 1968774 (Ill. C.A.) 7

Huggins v. Citibank, N.A., S.E.2d 275, 2003 WL 21910366, (Sup. Ct., S.C. 2003) 133

I

Intel Corporation v. Hamidi, 30 Cal. 4th 1342 (Cal. Sup. Ct. 2003) ... 162

K

Kanitz v. Rogers Cable Inc., [2002] O.J. No. 665, 58 O.R. (3d) 299 (S.C.J.) 6, 7, 24

L

Lac Minerals Ltd. v. International Corona Resources, [1989] S.C.J. No. 83, [1989] 2 S.C.R. 574 133

Lipiec v. Borsa, [1996] O.J. No. 3819, 31 C.C.L.T. (2d) 294 (Gen. Div.) 164

N

National Bank of Canada v. Clifford Chance, [1996] O.J. No. 3251, 30 O.R. (3d) 746 (Gen. Div.) 4

O

Ontario (Attorney General) v. Dieleman, [1994] O.J. No. 1864, 117 D.L.R. (4th) 449 (Gen. Div.) 164

P

Pharmaceutical Society of Great Britain v. Boots Cash Chemists (Southern) Ltd., [1953] 1 Q.B. 401 (C.A.) 3

R

R. v. Libman, [1985] S.C.J. No. 56,
[1985] 2 S.C.R. 178.................... 34

R. v. Théroux, [1993] S.C.J. No. 42,
[1993] 2 S.C.R. 5...................... 153

Robet v. Versus Brokerage Services
Inc. (c.o.b. E*Trade Canada),
[2001] O.J. No. 1341 (S.C.J.)....... 8

Rudder v. Microsoft Corp., [1999]
O.J. No. 3778, 47 C.C.L.T. (2d)
168 (S.C.J.)....................2, 5, 6, 24

S

Specht v. Netscape Communications
Corp., 150 F. Supp. 2d 585
(S.D.N.Y. 2002), affd 306 F. 3d
17 (2d Cir. 2002).......................... 8

Somwar v. McDonald's Restaurants
Canada Ltd. [2006] O.J. No. 64
(S.C.J.).................................... 164

Sotelo v. DirectRevenue, LLC 384
F. Supp 2d 1219 (N.D. Ill.
2005) 163

T

Thomas Kerrins v. Intermix Media,
No. 2:05-cv-05408-RGK-SS
(C.D. Cal. 2006)...................... 163

Tilden Rent-a-Car Co. v. Clendenning
(1978), 83 D.L.R. (3d) 400 (Ont.
C.A.)... 5

W

Williams v. America Online, Inc.,
43 UCC Rep. Serv. 3d 1101
(Mass. Sup. Ct. 2001)................... 6

Y

Yahoo! Inc. v. La Ligue Contre le
Racisme et L'Antisemitisme,
169 F. Supp. 2d 1181 (N.D. Cal.
2001).. 34

Z

Z.I. Pompey Industrie v. ECU-Line
N.V., [2003] S.C.J. No. 23,
[2003] 1 S.C.R. 450..................... 6

Zhu v. Merrill Lynch HSBC, [2002]
B.C.J. No. 2883, [2002] B.C.P.C.
535.. 8

INTRODUCTION

Perhaps it is self-evident and trite to state that the Internet has forced us to revisit and sometimes re-conceptualize established legal principles. Sometimes the Internet functions solely as a communications medium to which existing rules can easily be applied. Sometimes it requires those rules to be clarified and enhanced. And sometimes the Internet raises novel issues that cannot be adequately captured by existing norms.

It may be trite, but it is also true. The subject of online consumer protection, perhaps more than any other legal topic, illustrates all three positions. The Internet has also expanded our notions of consumer protection beyond the traditional concepts of buyer protection inherent in Canadian consumer protection legislation that predates the cyber era. The many facets of online consumer protection comprise the subject of this book, part of the "Information Technology Law in Canada" series.

The principal difficulty in writing this book has been delineating the boundaries of what is meant by consumer protection in the online environment. Are privacy and security of personal information consumer protection issues? Perhaps not traditionally, but the vast collection of personal information through technological means, and the apparent violability of that information as evidenced by several well-publicized security breaches, have made these issues particularly important to consumers.

Scams and schemes that target consumers make use of the Internet to target victims to an extent that was not formerly possible. "Phishing" has become a consumer concern that threatens to erode consumer confidence in legitimate electronic commerce. The proliferation of "spam" is a consumer issue, not only because it clogs our mailboxes and slows our operating systems, but also because spammers are frequently engaged in criminal-like behaviour that targets consumers.

Is music downloading a consumer issue? One would not have thought that copying music before the advent of the Internet was something that was deserving of serious evaluation from a consumer rights perspective. But the inadequacy of existing copyright legislation when applied to the online context, coupled with perceived abuses by both creators and users, have highlighted for some the need for special forms of consumer protection. For example, when is an Internet service provider permitted to release a subscriber's personal information to a rights holder intent on pursuing legal options?

Where does all this leave conventional notions of consumer protection? Are online consumers still concerned about traditional warranties and remedies? Do they care that the "distance sale" nature of most online purchases renders those traditional protections ineffectual? Or have these new concerns replaced the rather mundane problems of receiving what was paid for?

I fear that there is a disconnect between the realities of the practical issues facing the online consumer and the questions that are receiving the bulk of attention from the media and academics. At a recent conference presentation, I lamented the fact that an online consumer protection harmonization effort by the provinces and territories of Canada was not proceeding as it should, with the result that consumers in some provincial or territorial jurisdictions did not receive the right to receive credit card charge-backs when their sales contracts were cancelled in the appropriate circumstances. A law professor in the audience prefaced his question by stating "Who cares about credit card charge-backs?" and suggested the more important and interesting Internet-related consumer issue was the free dissemination of content.

While it is true that the Internet raises several original consumer issues and challenges some established norms, it is also a medium over which a significant amount of traditional commerce is conducted. The online consumer in Saskatchewan who lacks a practical recourse against a deceptive overseas seller, or the consumer in Ontario who is forced to litigate his or her legitimate $100 claim in the State of Washington could be forgiven for feeling that online consumer protection rights have been lost in the frenzy over rights to access content freely.

This book unapologetically examines online consumer protection in Canada from the traditional buyer/seller rights and obligations perspectives. But it also tackles some of those novel issues (insofar as they are also consumer concerns) that are at the forefront of both the popular media's focus and much academic discourse, as the Internet has inarguably broadened the concept of consumer protection. Inevitably, some choices had to be made. These choices reflect the author's particular interests, and flow logically and consequentially from traditional concepts of consumer protection law. Much has been written already about downloading of music. A comprehensive focus on intellectual property laws in the consumer context is the topic of another book.

Finally, as most consumer protection law is the result of legislation, inevitably there will be amendments and additions over the shelf-life of this volume. Indeed, legislation on issues such as spam and identity theft may be forthcoming. The discussion in this book reflects the state of the law as of mid-2006.

1

THE ELECTRONIC CONTRACT

Consumer agreements entered into online are, fundamentally, commercial contracts. Accordingly, the private law of contract will generally apply to all consumer agreements, insofar as private law principles have not been altered by legislation directed at the distinctive character of consumer contracts. The starting point for any examination of the enforceability of an online consumer agreement therefore must be the application of the principles of contract law. Additionally, because the focus of our examination is the medium of the Internet, the application and clarification of contractual principles with respect to the online environment, through judicial decisions and new legislation, must also be evaluated.

An examination of the general tenets of contract law is obviously beyond the scope of this book. However, an assessment of recent developments relating to online contract formation and enforcement is essential to a discussion of online consumer protection, as these developments clearly are relevant to online consumer agreements, and indeed frequently have the greatest impact in the business-to-consumer context.

I. FORMATION OF ONLINE CONTRACTS

In 1999 the Uniform Law Conference of Canada adopted the *Uniform Electronic Commerce Act ("UECA")*,[1] which is based on international standards relating to contracting over open electronic networks.[2] The *UECA* has influenced the development of electronic commerce legislation in most provincial and territorial jurisdictions in Canada.[3] These relatively new rules tackle many, but certainly not all, of the problematic questions relating to the application of established common law and civil law principles of contract to the online environment. Electronic commerce legislation now generally provides for

---

[1]   Reproduced in Appendix I to this chapter, and available online: <http://www.ulcc.ca>.

[2]   See UNCITRAL Model Law on Electronic Commerce (1996), online: <http://www.uncitral.org>.

[3]   Some jurisdictions have legislation almost identical to the *UECA* (*e.g.*, Nova Scotia). Others are clearly influenced by the *UECA*. Only Quebec's legislation is very different, although there are some similarities.

electronic equivalence of written and electronic communications, and establishes some of the rules governing the formation of electronic contracts.

The following discussion will highlight several of the peculiar issues relating to contracting over the Internet, and will focus especially on the application of these rules to the online consumer agreement. Despite the *UECA*'s influence on the development of electronic commerce legislation in Canada, uniformity, unhappily, has not been realized. Consequently, where a particular rule relating to electronic contract formation arises, reference will be made for the purposes of consistency to the relevant provision of the *UECA*.[4]

The *UECA* and its counterparts expressly allow for electronic forms of communication in contract formation.[5] Except possibly in Quebec,[6] there is no longer any doubt that so-called "click-wrap" contracts are enforceable in Canada. The *UECA* specifically states that interactive means such as touching or "clicking" an appropriately designated icon or place on a computer screen can constitute offer or acceptance or can be used to express any other matter that is material to the formation or operation of a contract.[7] There is also judicial authority in Canada that suggests that even under common law principles electronic actions can have legal contractual implications.[8] From the consumer's perspective, there may not be any argument that the online culture of surfing and clicking does not amount to the "meeting of the minds" necessary to form a binding business to consumer contract. Indeed, the Ontario Superior

---

[4]   For a sectional concordance of the *UECA* with provincial and territorial electronic commerce legislation in Canada, see T. Scassa and M. Deturbide, *Electronic Commerce and Internet Law in Canada* (Toronto: CCH Canadian Limited, 2004) at 27 *et seq.*

[5]   See for example *UECA*, s. 20(2).

[6]   A 2005 decision of the Court of Quebec evaluated whether "clicking" constituted acceptance of an online contract, and concluded that something more than a mere click is required to demonstrate a clear mental intention. See *Aspencer1.com v. Paysystems Corp.*, [2005] J.Q. No. 1573 (C.Q. Civ.).

It has been suggested that the court did not have to comment on the enforceability of "clicking" to decide the case, which did not actually involve interactive acceptance by "clicking"; that the court's comments were contrary to previous jurisprudence from Quebec and Canadian common law jurisdictions; and that the low level of the court that rendered the decision will limit its jurisprudential value. See C. Morgan, "I Click, You Click, We all Click ... But Do We Have a Contract?: A Case Comment on *Aspencer1.com v. Paysystems*" (2005) 4 C.J.L.T. 109.

[7]   *UECA*, s. 20(1).

[8]   See *Rudder v. Microsoft Corp.*, [1999] O.J. No. 3778, 47 C.C.L.T. (2d) 168 (S.C.J.).

Court has signalled that clicking "I agree" will have legal consequences analogous to the "sanctity" that must be given to written agreements.[9]

It is also clear that interactions with electronic agents can result in binding contracts.[10] Whether in fact such an interaction constitutes the elements necessary to form a contract depends on whether the communication from the electronic agent can be considered an offer, acceptance, or something else. Electronic agents can only operate within pre-set parameters, so much will depend on the factual circumstances of the interaction.[11]

A.   Offer and Invitation to Treat

The *UECA* clearly states that an offer may be made electronically.[12] The question of whether a price list or advertisement on a Web site constitutes an offer or a mere invitation to treat generally requires the application of well-established legal principles, which would suggest that such a list or advertisement would in most cases be simply an invitation to conduct business.[13] Much will depend on factual circumstances. For example, a Web site may make it explicit that its content does not constitute an offer capable of being accepted without some further contemplation by the vendor.

B.   Acceptance

The issue of when and where acceptance occurs in the online environment will determine whether an enforceable legal agreement has been formed, and if it has, will influence the jurisdictional issues with respect to the contract. According to the *UECA*, an electronic document is

---

[9] *Ibid.*

[10] *UECA*, s. 21 states:

   A contract may be formed by the interaction of an electronic agent and a natural person or by the interaction of electronic agents.

[11] See discussion on offer and acceptance, *infra.*

[12] *UECA*, s. 20(1).

[13] See, for example, *Pharmaceutical Society of Great Britain v. Boots Cash Chemists (Southern) Ltd.*, [1953] 1 Q.B. 401 (C.A.). In the electronic contracting context specifically, the United Nations Convention on International Trade Law's ("UNCITRAL") Model Convention on Electronic Commerce states that an offer of goods or services via the Internet is to be regarded, unless otherwise provided, as an invitation to make an offer. The notes to the Convention indicate that this is analogous to the rule established in traditional media. Online: <http://www.uncitral.org>.

sent when it enters an information system outside the control of the originator, and an electronic document is *received* by the addressee when it enters the information system designated or used by the addressee and is capable of being retrieved and processed by the address.[14] What the *UECA* does not stipulate, however, is whether or not acceptance rules established by common law, such as the mailbox rule which states that acceptance occurs when the letter addressed to the offeror is placed in a mailbox, apply to online communications. The *UECA* provides guidance as to when an offer has been received (when it enters the addressee's information system). It does not state that such receipt constitutes acceptance.

Instantaneous communications are generally not subject to the mailbox rule;[15] rather, acceptance occurs when the communications are received by the offeror. Yet the technology of Internet communications means that they often cannot be regarded as "instantaneous". Communications may be routed through several servers that potentially could block messages, and even intended recipients can employ technological measures such as spam filters to prevent delivery of some electronic communications.

As of this writing, the issue of when acceptance occurs with respect to online communications remains unresolved. The importance of this issue to online consumers may be diminished by explicit terms on vendor Web sites that stipulate the mechanics of acceptance. In many online consumer transactions, "tracking" or "reference" numbers will not signify acceptance of a putative purchaser's offer, but merely an acknowledgment of receipt of the offer. Acceptance occurs when the vendor subsequently communicates acceptance, usually by electronic mail. The terms on the Web site may also indicate that acceptance crystallizes when the message is sent from the vendor's information system.[16] The insertion of such explicit terms is an illustration of the common practice, in the context of Internet legal issues, of the marketplace's attempt to eliminate uncertainties.

---

[14] *UECA*, s. 23. If the addressee has not designated or does not use an information system for the purpose of receiving documents of the type sent, the electronic document is presumed to be received when the addressee becomes aware of the document in the addressee's information system and the document is capable of being retrieved and processed.

[15] See, for example, *National Bank of Canada v. Clifford Chance*, [1996] O.J. No. 3251, 30 O.R. (3d) 746 (Gen. Div.).

[16] See Lisa K. Abe and Marie-Helene Constantin, *Web Law: Agreements, Guidelines and Use Policies* (Markham, Ont.: Butterworths, 2005) at 96:

Given that, in Canada, the mailbox rule ... will likely apply to online contracts that are not instantaneous, the acceptance of any offer must be communicated to the offeror. By sending a clear statement to the Internet user that a Web site agreement has been successfully completed ... it will likely be held to be binding.

II.   NOTICE OF TERMS

Most online consumer contracts are contracts of adhesion,[17] that is, they are of a standard form that provides little or no opportunity for the consumer to negotiate terms. In theory, consumers should therefore have the terms of click-wrap agreements presented unambiguously, and onerous terms should specifically be brought to the consumer's attention.[18]

Under the *Civil Code of Quebec* ("C.C.Q."), an abusive clause in a contract of adhesion will be void.[19] Courts in Canada have also held that onerous provisions must be drawn to the attention of the other party by the party seeking to rely on them.[20] Yet in the online context, Ontario courts have refused to entertain any consideration of unconscionability in circumstances that arguably presented onerous conditions to consumers. Rather, the overriding concern of the courts in these cases appears to focus on commercial certainty in the online environment.

A.   Click-Wrap Agreements

In *Rudder v. Microsoft Corp.*[21] a claim was brought under Ontario's *Class Proceedings Act, 1992*[22] on behalf of subscribers to Microsoft Corporation's MSN Internet service. The claim sought damages against MSN for allegedly overcharging members' credit cards.

Subscribers were required to "electronically execute" an agreement, only a portion of which could be viewed at any one time, by clicking an "I agree" icon. One of the provisions of the agreement stated:

---

[17] See John Yogis, *Canadian Law Dictionary*, 4th ed. (Hauppauge, New York: Barron's, 1998) at 9:

> Usually a contract in standard form prepared by one party and submitted to the other on a take-it-or-leave-it basis. It implies a grave inequality in bargaining power ...

[18] There is also an argument that online contracts raise peculiar issues related to the "culture" of online buying that necessitate even stronger cognizance of the inequality of bargaining power, especially in the consumer context. See Teresa Scassa and Michael Deturbide, *Electronic Commerce and Internet Law in Canada* (Toronto: CCH Canadian, 2004) at 11.

[19] Article 1437 C.C.Q. See C. Morgan, "I Click, You Click, We all Click ... But Do We Have a Contract?: A Case Comment on Aspencer1.com v. Paysystems" (2005) 4 C.J.L.T. 109 for a discussion of the application of the Quebec *Civil Code* to a click-wrap contract.

[20] See, for example, *Tilden Rent-a-Car Co. v. Clendenning* (1978), 83 D.L.R. (3d) 400 (Ont. C.A.).

[21] [1999] O.J. No. 3778, 47 C.C.L.T. (2d) 168 (S.C.J.).

[22] S.O. 1992, c. 6.

> This Agreement is governed by the laws of the State of Washington, U.S.A., and you consent to the exclusive jurisdiction and venue of courts in King County, Washington, in all disputes arising out of or relating to your use of MSN or your MSN membership.

The Ontario Superior Court did not agree that the clause was analogous to the "fine print" of a paper-based contract. The standard that the court applied was that the clause needed to be "aberrant" before there could be any consideration of striking it. Any notion of unconscionability was ignored due to a perceived need for online commercial certainty and a concern about undermining the efficiency of electronic commerce. The facts that Ontario consumers were unlikely to travel to the State of Washington to dispute small claims, and that Canadian consumers were excluded from their domestic legal system, were disregarded.

Although the Supreme Court of Canada has often indicated that forum selection clauses are generally enforceable, this view assumes a meeting of the minds on the contract's terms. The Supreme Court has also stated that forum selection clauses may be unconscionable,[23] and courts in the United States have examined such clauses for their prominence of placement and consumer protection consequences.[24]

It is possible that the facts in *Rudder* would have resulted in the same outcome if notice and unconscionability issues were fully evaluated by the court. Nevertheless, it is the court's lack of concern for the consequences to the online consumer and its failure to recognize the adequate notice and bargaining power issues inherent in online standard form contracts that are troubling from a consumer protection perspective.

Even more disconcerting for consumers was a subsequent decision of the Ontario Superior Court that found it was reasonable for an online vendor to give notice of amendments to its user agreement by posting changes to the vendor's Web site. According to the court in *Kanitz v. Rogers Cable Inc.*,[25] it was not unreasonable for persons who buy goods and services online "to have the legal attributes of their relationship with the very entity that is providing such electronic access, defined and communicated to them through that electronic format".[26] Hence, a mandatory arbitration clause added to the defendant's Web site with no other notice to consumers was held to be valid and a class action suit

---

[23] See, for example, *Z.I. Pompey Industrie v. ECU-Line N.V.*, [2003] S.C.J. No. 23, [2003] 1 S.C.R. 450.

[24] See, for example, *Williams v. America Online, Inc.*, 43 UCC Rep. Serv. 3d 1101 (Mass. Sup. Ct. 2001); *America Online, Inc. v. Mendoza*, 90 Cal. App. 4th 1 (2001).

[25] [2002] O.J. No. 665, 58 O.R. (3d) 299 (S.C.J.).

[26] *Ibid.*, at para. 32.

stayed because the original user agreement provided that such notice could be provided.

Again, one could arguably reach such a conclusion on a set of facts where adequate consumer notice was addressed. But in the *Kanitz* case the user agreement was not manifestly presented on Rogers' customer support Web site, and no other notice of amendment was highlighted. The court concluded that it took a review of "only" five screens to get to the amended user agreement. Although the court conceded that more could have been done to bring the amendment to the attention of subscribers, it also felt that because subscribers had agreed to have their legal relations changed in this way, it was not unreasonable to expect them to periodically review the vendor's Web site to check for amendments to the user agreement.

Such reasoning is more easily understandable in law in a business-to-business context. In a business-to-consumer contract, surely some consumer protection considerations would be appropriate (despite the fact that any application of consumer protection legislation was not raised). The court in *Kanitz* had little sympathy towards Rogers' customers. Although the court accepted that this was clearly a case of inadequate bargaining power, it was not prepared to find that the agreements were improvident. Nor did lack of notice disturb the court:

> I do not accept that the customer can reasonably assert that all he or she should have to do is simply go to the main screen of the defendant's web site and expect to find a notice regarding any such amendments. The defendant is a large company with many different interests, all of which are represented on its web site.[27]

The court gave little consideration to the peculiarities of consumer buying in the online environment, or the practical effect of the arbitration clause. Again, it is interesting to note the different approach taken by some American courts in similar circumstances, where a contextual analysis had resulted in findings that such arbitration clauses could be unconscionable.[28] Ontario's recently proclaimed *Consumer Protection Act, 2002* now prevents unilateral changes that would require that consumer agreements be submitted to arbitration.[29] However, "be careful

---

[27] *Ibid.*, at para. 24.

[28] See, for example, *Comb v. PayPal, Inc.*, 218 F. Supp. 2d 1165 (N.D. Cal. 2002); *Hubbert v. Dell Corp.*, 2005 WL 1968774 (Ill. C.A.) in which an arbitration requirement was upheld, but only after the court considered whether it would be unconscionable to do so.

[29] S.O. 2002, c. 30, Sch. A, ss. 7, 8.

what you click" is a truism that unmistakably emerges from these "click-wrap" cases in Ontario.

Ironically, courts in Ontario have had less difficulty in finding that literal disclaimer clauses (as opposed to forum selection or arbitration clauses designed to limit liability to consumers) were not enforceable in circumstances of online trading. For example, the Ontario Superior Court concluded that a disclaimer clause that removed all liability for inaccuracy of information of an Internet stock trading service meant that there could not have been a meeting of the minds of customer and broker.[30] Similarly, the British Columbia Provincial Court found that a disclaimer that removed liability for inaccuracy reserved the right of the broker to be grossly negligent, and was consequently unenforceable.[31]

B.   Browse-Wrap Agreements

In situations where consumers do not affirmatively agree to terms, by clicking "I Agree" or a similar icon, it would be much more difficult for a vendor to assert that the consumer is bound by an online agreement. So-called "browse-wrap" agreements have not been considered by Canadian courts, although federal courts in the United States have held that consumers would not be subject to an arbitration clause in circumstances where the licence agreement was presented but was not specifically assented to.[32] Situations where terms are contained on a sub-page accessible by clicking a hyperlink, or where the act of downloading is meant to indicate acceptance of licence terms, lack the specificity of acknowledgment that the courts appear to be seeking. Most vendor Web sites consequently require that consumers take a confirmatory action, such as clicking, to denote explicit consent to the vendor's terms.

---

[30] *Robet v. Versus Brokerage Services Inc. (c.o.b. E*Trade Canada)*, [2001] O.J. No. 1341 (S.C.J.).

[31] *Zhu v. Merrill Lynch HSBC*, [2002] B.C.J. No. 2883, [2002] B.C.P.C. 535.

[32] See *Specht v. Netscape Communications Corp.*, 150 F. Supp. 2d 585 (S.D.N.Y. 2002), affd 306 F. 3d 17 (2d Cir. 2002).

Appendix I

UNIFORM ELECTRONIC COMMERCE ACT

(adopted by the Uniform Law Conference of Canada)

Definitions

1. The definitions in this section apply in this Act.

(a)   "electronic" includes created, recorded, transmitted or stored in digital form or in other intangible form by electronic, magnetic or optical means or by any other means that has capabilities for creation, recording, transmission or storage similar to those means and "electronically" has a corresponding meaning.

(b)   "electronic signature" means information in electronic form that a person has created or adopted in order to sign a document and that is in, attached to or associated with the document .

(c)   "Government" means

    (i)   the Government of [enacting jurisdiction];

    (ii)   any department, agency or body of the Government of [enacting jurisdiction], [other than Crown Corporations incorporated by or under a law of [enacting jurisdiction]]; and

    [(iii)   any city, metropolitan authority, town, village, township, district or [rural municipality or other municipal body, however designated, incorporated or established by or under a law of [enacting jurisdiction].]

Application

2. (1) Subject to this section, this Act applies in respect of [enacting jurisdiction] law.

(2) The [appropriate authority] may, by [statutory instrument], specify provisions of or requirements under [enacting jurisdiction] law in respect of which this Act does not apply.

(3) This Act does not apply in respect of

(a)   wills and their codicils;

(b)   trusts created by wills or by codicils to wills;

(c)   powers of attorney, to the extent that they are in respect of the financial affairs or personal care of an individual;

(d)   documents that create or transfer interests in land and that require registration to be effective against third parties.

(4) Except for Part 3, this Act does not apply in respect of negotiable instruments, including negotiable documents of title.

(5) Nothing in this Act limits the operation of any provision of [enacting jurisdiction] law that expressly authorizes, prohibits or regulates the use of electronic documents.

(6) The [appropriate authority] may, by [statutory instrument], amend subsection (3) to add any document or class of documents, or to remove any document or class of documents previously added under this subsection.

(7) For the purpose of subsection (5), the use of words and expressions like "in writing" and "signature" and other similar words and expressions does not by itself prohibit the use of electronic documents.

Crown

3. This Act binds the Crown.

Interpretation

4. The provisions of this Act relating to the satisfaction of a requirement of law apply whether the law creates an obligation or provides consequences for doing something or for not doing something.

PART 1
PROVISION AND RETENTION OF INFORMATION

Legal recognition

5. Information shall not be denied legal effect or enforceability solely by reason that it is in electronic form.

Use not mandatory

6. (1) Nothing in this Act requires a person to use or accept information in electronic form, but a person's consent to do so may be inferred from the person's conduct.

(2) Despite subsection (1), the consent of the Government to accept information in electronic form may not be inferred by its conduct but must be expressed by communication accessible to the public or to those likely to communicate with it for particular purposes.

Requirement for information to be in writing

7. A requirement under [enacting jurisdiction] law that information be in writing is satisfied by information in electronic form if the information is accessible so as to be usable for subsequent reference.

Providing information in writing

8. (1) A requirement under [enacting jurisdiction] law for a person to provide information in writing to another person is satisfied by the provision of the information in an electronic document,

  (a) if the electronic document that is provided to the other person is accessible by the other person and capable of being retained by the other person so as to be usable for subsequent reference, and

  (b) where the information is to be provided to the Government, if

    (i) the Government or the part of Government to which the information is to be provided has consented to accept electronic documents in satisfaction of the requirement; and

    (ii) the electronic document meets the information technology standards and acknowledgement rules, if any, established by the Government or part of Government, as the case may be.

Providing information in specific form

9. A requirement under [enacting jurisdiction] law for a person to provide information to another person in a specified non-electronic form is satisfied by the provision of the information in an electronic document,

  (a) if the information is provided in the same or substantially the same form and the electronic document is accessible by the other person and capable of being retained by the other person so as to be usable for subsequent reference, and

  (b) where the information is to be provided to the Government, if

    (i) the Government or the part of Government to which the information is to be provided has consented to accept electronic documents in satisfaction of the requirement; and

(ii)   the electronic document meets the information technology standards and acknowledgement rules, if any, established by the Government or part of Government, as the case may be.

Signatures

10. (1) A requirement under [enacting jurisdiction] law for the signature of a person is satisfied by an electronic signature.

(2) For the purposes of subsection (1), the [authority responsible for the requirement] may make a regulation that,

(a)   the electronic signature shall be reliable for the purpose of identifying the person, in the light of all the circumstances, including any relevant agreement and the time the electronic signature was made; and

(b)   the association of the electronic signature with the relevant electronic document shall be reliable for the purpose for which the electronic document was made, in the light of all the circumstances, including any relevant agreement and the time the electronic signature was made.

(3) For the purposes of subsection (1), where the signature or signed document is to be provided to the Government, the requirement is satisfied only if

(a)   the Government or the part of Government to which the information is to be provided has consented to accept electronic signatures; and

(b)   the electronic document meets the information technology standards and requirements as to method and as to reliability of the signature, if any, established by the Government or part of Government, as the case may be.

Provision of originals

11. (1) A requirement under [enacting jurisdiction] law that requires a person to present or retain a document in original form is satisfied by the provision or retention of an electronic document if

(a)   there exists a reliable assurance as to the integrity of the information contained in the electronic document from the time the document to be presented or retained was first made in its final form, whether as a paper document or as an electronic document;

(b)   where the document in original form is to be provided to a person, the electronic document that is provided to the person is accessible by the person and capable of being retained by the person so as to be usable for subsequent reference; and

(c)   where the document in original form is to be provided to the Government,

    (i)   the Government or the part of Government to which the information is to be provided has consented to accept electronic documents in satisfaction of the requirement; and

    (ii)   the electronic document meets the information technology standards and acknowledgement rules, if any, established by the Government or part of Government, as the case may be.

(2) For the purpose of paragraph (1)(a),

(a)   the criterion for assessing integrity is whether the information has remained complete and unaltered, apart from the introduction of any changes that arise in the normal course of communication, storage and display;

(b)   the standard of reliability required shall be assessed in the light of the purpose for which the document was made and in the light of all the circumstances.

Whether document is capable of being retained

12. An electronic document is deemed not to be capable of being retained if the person providing the electronic document inhibits the printing or storage of the electronic document by the recipient.

Retention of documents

13. A requirement under [enacting jurisdiction] law to retain a document is satisfied by the retention of an electronic document if

(a)   the electronic document is retained in the format in which it was made, sent or received, or in a format that does not materially change the information contained in the document that was originally made, sent or received;

(b)   the information in the electronic document will be accessible so as to be usable for subsequent reference by any person who is entitled to have access to the document or who is authorized to require its production; and

(c) where the electronic document was sent or received, information, if any, that identifies the origin and destination of the electronic document and the date and time when it was sent or received is also retained.

Copies

14. Where a document may be submitted in electronic form, a requirement under a provision of [enacting jurisdiction] law for one or more copies of a document to be submitted to a single addressee at the same time is satisfied by the submission of a single version of an electronic document.

Other requirements continue to apply

15. Nothing in this Part limits the operation of any requirement under [enacting jurisdiction] law for information to be posted or displayed in a specified manner or for any information or document to be transmitted by a specified method.

Authority to prescribe forms and manner of filing forms

16. (1) If a provision of [enacting jurisdiction] law requires a person to communicate information, the minister of the Crown responsible for the provision may prescribe electronic means to be used for the communication of the information and the use of those means satisfies that requirement.

(2) If a statute of [enacting jurisdiction] sets out a form, the [authority responsible for the form] may make an electronic form that is substantially the same as the form set out in the statute and the electronic form is to be considered as the form set out in the statute.

(3) A provision of [enacting jurisdiction] law that authorizes the prescription of a form or the manner of filing a form includes the authority to prescribe an electronic form or electronic means of filing the form, as the case may be.

(4) The definitions in this subsection apply in this section.

(a) "filing" includes all manner of submitting, regardless of how it is designated.

(b) "prescribe" includes all manner of issuing, making and establishing, regardless of how it is designated.

Collection, storage, etc.

17. (1) In the absence of an express provision in any [enacting jurisdiction] law that electronic means may not be used or that they must be used in specified ways, a minister of the Crown in right of [enacting jurisdiction] or an entity referred to in subparagraphs 1(c)(ii) [or (iii)] may use electronic means to create, collect, receive, store, transfer, distribute, publish or otherwise deal with documents or information.

(2) For the purpose of subsection (1), the use of words and expressions like "in writing" and "signature" and other similar words and expressions does not by itself constitute an express provision that electronic means may not be used.

Electronic payments

18. (1) A payment that is authorized or required to be made to the Government under [enacting jurisdiction] law may be made in electronic form in any manner specified by [the Receiver General] for the [enacting jurisdiction].

(2) A payment that is authorized or required to be made by the Government may be made in electronic form in any manner specified by the [Receiver General] for the [enacting jurisdiction].

PART 2
COMMUNICATION OF ELECTRONIC DOCUMENTS

Definition of "electronic agent"

19. In this Part, "electronic agent" means a computer program or any electronic means used to initiate an action or to respond to electronic documents or actions in whole or in part without review by a natural person at the time of the response or action.

Formation and operation of contracts

20. (1) Unless the parties agree otherwise, an offer or the acceptance of an offer, or any other matter that is material to the formation or operation of a contract, may be expressed

    (a)   by means of an electronic document; or

    (b)   by an action in electronic form, including touching or clicking on an appropriately designated icon or place on a computer screen or otherwise communicating electronically in a manner that is intended to express the offer, acceptance or other matter.

(2) A contract shall not be denied legal effect or enforceability solely by reason that an electronic document was used in its formation.

Involvement of electronic agents

21. A contract may be formed by the interaction of an electronic agent and a natural person or by the interaction of electronic agents.

Errors when dealing with electronic agents

22. An electronic document made by a natural person with the electronic agent of another person has no legal effect and is not enforceable if the natural person made a material error in the document and

(a)   the electronic agent did not provide the natural person with an opportunity to prevent or correct the error;

(b)   the natural person notifies the other person of the error as soon as practicable after the natural person learns of the error and indicates that he or she made an error in the electronic document;

(c)   the natural person takes reasonable steps, including steps that conform to the other person's instructions to return the consideration received, if any, as a result of the error or, if instructed to do so, to destroy the consideration; and

(d)   the natural person has not used or received any material benefit or value from the consideration, if any, received from the other person.

Time and place of sending and receipt of electronic documents

23. (1) Unless the originator and the addressee agree otherwise, an electronic document is sent when it enters an information system outside the control of the originator or, if the originator and the addressee are in the same information system, when it becomes capable of being retrieved and processed by the addressee.

(2) An electronic document is presumed to be received by the addressee,

(a)   when it enters an information system designated or used by the addressee for the purpose of receiving documents of the type sent and it is capable of being retrieved and processed by the addressee; or

(b)   if the addressee has not designated or does not use an information system for the purpose of receiving documents of the type sent, when the addressee becomes aware of the electronic document in the addressee's information system and the electronic document is capable of being of being retrieved and processed by the addressee.

(3) Unless the originator and the addressee agree otherwise, an electronic document is deemed to be sent from the originator's place of business and is deemed to be received at the addressee's place of business.

(4) For the purposes of subsection (3)

(a)   if the originator or the addressee has more than one place of business, the place of business is that which has the closest relationship to the underlying transaction to which the electronic document relates or, if there is no underlying transaction, the principal place of business of the originator or the addressee; and

(b)   if the originator or the addressee does not have a place of business, the references to "place of business" in subsection (3) are to be read as references to "habitual residence".

PART 3
CARRIAGE OF GOODS

Actions related to contracts of carriage of goods

24. This Part applies to any action in connection with a contract of carriage of goods, including, but not limited to,

(a)   furnishing the marks, number, quantity or weight of goods;
(b)   stating or declaring the nature or value of goods;
(c)   issuing a receipt for goods;
(d)   confirming that goods have been loaded;
(e)   giving instructions to a carrier of goods;
(f)   claiming delivery of goods;
(g)   authorizing release of goods;
(h)   giving notice of loss of, or damage to, goods;
(i)   undertaking to deliver goods to a named person or a person authorized to claim delivery;
(j)   granting, acquiring, renouncing, surrendering, transferring or negotiating rights in goods;
(k)   notifying a person of terms and conditions of a contract of carriage of goods;

(l)   giving a notice or statement in connection with the performance of a contract of carriage of goods; and

(m)   acquiring or transferring rights and obligations under a contract of carriage of goods.

Documents

25. (1) Subject to subsection (2), a requirement under [enacting jurisdiction] law that an action referred to in any of paragraphs 24(a) to (m) be carried out in writing or by using a paper document is satisfied if the action is carried out by using one or more electronic documents.

(2) If a right is to be granted to or an obligation is to be acquired by one person and no other person and a provision of [enacting jurisdiction] law requires that, in order to do so, the right or obligation must be conveyed to that person by the transfer or use of a document in writing, that requirement is satisfied if the right or obligation is conveyed through the use of one or more electronic documents created by a method that gives reliable assurance that the right or obligation has become the right or obligation of that person and no other person.

(3) For the purposes of subsection (2), the standard of reliability required shall be assessed in the light of the purpose for which the right or obligation was conveyed and in the light of all the circumstances, including any relevant agreement.

(4) If one or more electronic documents are used to accomplish an action referred to in paragraph 24(j) or (m), no document in writing used to effect the action is valid unless the use of electronic documents has been terminated and replaced by the use of documents in writing. A document in writing issued in these circumstances must contain a statement of the termination, and the replacement of the electronic documents by documents in writing does not affect the rights or obligations of the parties involved.

(5) If a rule of [enacting jurisdiction] law is compulsorily applicable to a contract of carriage of goods that is set out in, or is evidenced by, a document in writing, that rule shall not be inapplicable to a contract of carriage of goods that is evidenced by one or more electronic documents by reason of the fact that the contract is evidenced by electronic documents instead of by a document in writing.

2

ONLINE CONSUMER PROTECTION LEGISLATION

Consumer protection legislation in Canada is a hodgepodge of mostly provincial statutes and regulations that attempt to provide various protections to buyers who purchase goods and services for their own personal use. Traditional consumer protection originated in the 1960s and 1970s, when governments recognized that consumers were virtually dependant on the fairness of those with whom they contracted for goods and services, and were consequently targets for exploitation.[1] Technological innovations such as the Internet have renewed efforts to examine the extent of consumer protection in the 21st century for the same reasons expressed in the 1960s and 1970s.

Ironically, the Internet rose in prominence at the very time that issues of consumer protection were receiving far less attention by governments. In the 1990s, consumer protection agencies were under-funded, and consumers were less concerned with consumer "rights".[2] Traditional consumer protection legislation — products of technologically simpler times, and which principally regulated credit transactions and conditions in sales agreements — did not deal adequately with online buying or the novel issues raised by new technologies.

Nevertheless, it should be made clear that traditional purchaser and consumer protection legislation continues to apply to online interactions. For example, legislative protections such as the implied warranties of "merchantability", "fitness for purpose", and (in the case of Quebec) "quality" will be applicable to goods purchased online.[3] Traditional

---

[1] See J. S. Ziegel, "The Future of Canadian Consumerism" (1973) 51 Can. Bar Rev. 191.

[2] J. Ziegel, "The Development of Canadian Consumer Law" in *Commercial and Consumer Transactions: Cases, Text and Materials*, 3rd ed. (Volume I, *Sales Transactions*) (Toronto: Emond Montgomery Publications, 1995) at 13.

[3] See, for example, the Ontario *Sale of Goods Act*, R.S.O. 1990, c. S.1, s. 13:

    13. In a contract of sale, unless the circumstances of the contract are such as to show a different intention, there is,

        (a)   an implied condition on the part of the seller that in the case of a sale the seller has a right to sell the goods, and that in the case of an agreement to sell the seller will have a right to sell the goods at the time when the property is to pass;

safeguards may be the only legislative protections in place in provincial jurisdictions that have not passed Internet-specific consumer protection laws. And in circumstances where online consumer protection legislation fails to tackle specific online consumer issues (such as "phishing", discussed in Chapter 3) the consumer is left with trying to adapt existing legislation to the particular problem.[4]

The purpose of this chapter is to focus on the recent efforts made in Canada that target online consumer protection. The broad application of the assortment of traditional federal and provincial sales laws to agreements, insofar as Internet sales agreements may also be captured by them, is the subject of traditional sales law, and is generally beyond the scope of this book.[5]

I.   HISTORY OF ONLINE CONSUMER PROTECTION IN CANADA

In 1998, the Office of Consumer Affairs, Industry Canada, commissioned a report that considered whether existing legislation was adequate to meet the needs of online consumers across Canada.[6] The report identified many outstanding questions, including issues relating to jurisdiction of online consumer contracts, whether a "cooling-off" period within which a consumer would be entitled to cancel a contract should be incorporated into online consumer agreements, and whether the mechanics of forming consumer agreements required clarification as to how and when a contract is formed online. The report also highlighted the

---

     (b)   an implied warranty that the buyer will have and enjoy quiet possession of the goods; and

     (c)   an implied warranty that the goods will be free from any charge or encumbrance in favour of any third party, not declared or known to the buyer before or at the time when the contract is made.

In Quebec, Art. 1726 C.C.Q. provides for a legal warranty of quality:

     1726. The seller is bound to warrant the buyer that the property and its accessories are, at the time of the sale, free of latent defects which render it unfit for the use for which it was intended or which so diminish its usefulness that the buyer would not have bought it or paid so high a price if he had been aware of them.

     The seller is not bound, however, to warrant against any latent defect known to the buyer or any apparent defect; an apparent defect is a defect that can be perceived by a prudent and diligent buyer without any need of expert assistance.

[4]   See, for example, the discussion of the application of the federal *Criminal Code*, R.S.C. 1985, c. C-46 and *Competition Act*, R.S.C. 1985, c. C-34 to identity theft, Chapter 3, *infra.*

[5]   For a discussion of sales legislation generally, see J. Ziegel, "The Development of Canadian Consumer Law" in *Commercial and Consumer Transactions: Cases, Text and Materials*, 3d ed. (Volume I, *Sales Transactions*) (Toronto: Emond Montgomery Publications, 1995).

[6]   Online: <http://www.chlc.ca/en/cls/index.cfm?sec=4&sub=4j>

fragmentation of consumer protection legislation across Canada, and questioned whether an effort at harmonization should be undertaken.

The first steps taken in relation to online consumer protection by the government of Canada did not address these issues directly. In keeping with the federal government's reluctance to regulate electronic commerce and its promotion of self-regulation, it advanced a voluntary system of good business practices in 1999 with the release of a Framework of "guiding principles of electronic commerce, especially as it pertains to transactions between consumers and vendors".[7] The Framework led to a voluntary code of practice, the *Canadian Code of Practice for Consumer Protection in Electronic Commerce*, which was "intended to establish benchmarks for good business practices for merchants conducting commercial activities with consumers online". But the Code clearly stipulated that it left "unchanged rights, remedies and other obligations that may exist as a result of consumer protection, privacy or other laws and regulations".[8] The Code addressed a variety of good business practices, including providing consumers with sufficient information to make informed choices, ensuring marketing practices are not misleading or deceptive, and ensuring that adequate disclosure is made before a consumer enters into an agreement.

It wasn't until 2001 that the idea of consumer protection legislation targeted at online consumers, and that addressed some of the questions in the 1998 Report, was reintroduced. In that year, the Consumer Measures Committee, a federal-provincial-territorial working group, released the *Internet Sales Contract Harmonization Template*[9] which, as its title suggests, sought to guide federal, provincial and territorial jurisdictions in realizing legislative uniformity with respect to online consumer protection. The *Template* has been endorsed by all federal, provincial, and territorial ministers responsible for consumer affairs, with the understanding that their respective jurisdictions would take action to implement legislation that reflected the *Template*'s framework. As of late 2006, five provinces have enacted new laws or made amendments to existing consumer protection legislation that reflects, to various degrees, the *Template*'s provisions.

---

[7]   "Principles of Consumer Protection for Electronic Commerce — A Canadian Framework". The Framework's principles "include consumer privacy, problem resolution, the transmission of commercial e-mail without consumer consent, and promoting consumer awareness on the safe use of electronic commerce". Online: <http://strategis.ic.gc.ca/principlese.pdf>.

[8]   Online: <http://strategis.ic.gc.ca/pics/ca/consumerprotection03.pdf>.

[9]   Online: <http://strategis.ic.gc.ca/pics/ca/sales_template.pdf> (hereinafter *Template*). The *Template* is reproduced at Appendix I.

II.   THE INTERNET SALES CONTRACT HARMONIZATION TEMPLATE

The *Template* modifies existing sales law in the online environment. Its focus is clearly on the rules relating to online buying and selling. In other words, the context of buying online is considered, and the traditional rules are amended to reflect that context. But the *Template* does not address new consumer issues that arise because of the medium of the Internet, such as "spyware", or conventional consumer issues outside the buying and selling context that have been exacerbated by the Internet, such as electronic junk mail or "spam". Indeed, the *Template* is even silent on the fundamental issue of jurisdiction.

The topics addressed by the *Template* may be classified into four headings: disclosure requirements of vendors before a consumer enters into an Internet sales contract; rules relating to formation of contracts online; circumstances in which consumers may be entitled to cancel an online agreement; and consumers' entitlement to credit card charge-backs.

Five provinces in Canada now have legislation that reflects the *Template*: Manitoba,[10] Alberta,[11] Nova Scotia,[12] Ontario,[13] and British Columbia.[14] Unfortunately, one of the prime inspirations for the development of the *Template*, that is, the harmonization of legislative efforts relating to online consumer protection, has not been achieved. For example, the information that must be disclosed before a consumer can enter into an online agreement is generally prescribed by regulation.[15] The Ontario legislation does not require credit card issuers to cancel credit card charges to the same extent as the *Template*.[16] Alberta's *Internet Sales Contract Regulation* addresses jurisdiction, providing broad application to Internet sales contracts in which the supplier or consumer is resident in Alberta, whereas the legislation in other provincial jurisdictions is silent on the issue.[17]

---

[10]   *Consumer Protection Act*, C.C.S.M., c. C200; *Internet Agreements Regulation,* Man. Reg. 176/2000.

[11]   *Fair Trading Act*, R.S.A. 2000, c. F-2; *Internet Sales Contract Regulation*, Alta. Reg. 81/2001.

[12]   *Consumer Protection Act*, R.S.N.S. 1989, c. 92; *Internet Sales Contract Regulations*, N.S. Reg. 91/2002.

[13]   *Consumer Protection Act, 2002*, S.O. 2002, c. 30; O. Reg. 17/05.

[14]   *Business Practices and Consumer Protection Act*, S.B.C. 2004, c. 2; *Consumer Contracts Regulations*, B.C. Reg. 272/2004.

[15]   For example, Ontario's *Consumer Protection Act, 2002*, S.O. 2002, s. 38.

[16]   *Ibid.*, s. 99.

[17]   Alta. Reg. 81/2001.

The following discussion considers the various protections provided by the *Template* in detail. The concordance between the provisions of the *Template* and the legislative provisions of the five provinces that have enacted some variation of the *Template* comprises Appendix II to this chapter. That Appendix also highlights those provisions where the provincial legislation deviates substantively from the *Template*. Thus, evaluation of the *Template* is incomplete without constant reference to the Concordance, which details how the *Template* has been implemented in specific legislation.

A.   Application of the *Template*

Although the *Template* stipulates that each jurisdiction that adopts it must determine its scope,[18] the *Template* is essentially designed to capture conventional buying and selling issues in a consumer context, and its definitions reflect those contained within traditional consumer protection legislation. A "consumer" is defined as an *individual* who receives or has the right to receive goods or services from a supplier[19] — that is, a person who in the course of the person's business provides goods or services to consumers. "Goods" and "services" must be used or provided primarily for personal, family or household purposes.[20] The *Template* applies to "internet sales contracts", defined as consumer transactions formed by text-based Internet communications.[21] Each jurisdiction that adopts the *Template* will likely need to modify these definitions to be in conformity with existing consumer protection legislation, but the substance of the *Template*'s application will be the online purchase of goods and services by consumers, for their personal use, from persons who sell to consumers in their course of business.

B.   Disclosure of Information

The *Template* requires that a supplier clearly disclose certain information to a consumer before an online contract is formed.[22] Failure to disclose this information may provide the consumer with a right of

---

[18]   Appendix I, s. 2.
[19]   *Ibid.*, s. 2.
[20]   *Ibid.*
[21]   *Ibid.*
[22]   *Ibid.*, s. 3(1)
        A supplier must make several types of disclosures before a consumer enters into an internet sales contract. See Appendix I.

cancellation[23] so online suppliers must take careful note of the disclosure requirements. Most of the requirements represent standard information that anyone would logically expect to be made known before entering into any contract, such as the supplier's name, business address, and phone number, and a fair and accurate description of the goods and services being sold. In recognition of its application to Internet transactions, the *Template* also requires the disclosure of the supplier's e-mail address, if available, and requires that the information be made accessible in a manner that ensures the consumer has accessed the information and is able to retain and print the information.[24]

The *Template* notably does not require explicit disclosure of forum selection, choice of law, or disclaimer clauses, except insofar as they are captured by the general requirements to disclose the terms and conditions of the contract,[25] or any other restrictions, limitations or conditions of purchase.[26] All information that must be disclosed pursuant to the *Template* must be prominently displayed in a clear and comprehensible manner.[27] Whether this requirement would aid consumers in circumstances reflected in cases like *Rudder v. Microsoft Corp.*[28] or *Kanitz v. Rogers Cable Inc.*[29] is unclear. The courts in those cases appeared to be satisfied that the allegedly "buried" terms were, in fact, clearly disclosed to the plaintiffs, although one could certainly argue that they were not highlighted "prominently".

The disclosure requirements in those jurisdictions that have online consumer protection legislation generally conform to those of the *Template,* although there are differences. For example, in Manitoba the *Internet Agreements Regulation* also requires sellers to disclose to consumers its policies for the protection of the consumer's financial and personal information.[30]

Related to disclosure, the *Template* specifies that a supplier must provide a consumer who enters into an Internet sales contract with a copy of the contract in writing or in electronic form within 15 days following the date on which the contract is entered into.[31] The contract must include the disclosure information discussed above, as well as the consumer's

---

[23]   *Ibid.*, s. 5(1).
[24]   *Ibid.*, ss. 3(1)(a)(iii); 3(2)(b).
[25]   *Ibid.*, s. 3(1)(a)(ix).
[26]   *Ibid.*, s. 3(1)(a)(xiii).
[27]   *Ibid.*, s. 3(2)(a).
[28]   [1999] O.J. No. 3778, 47 C.C.L.T. (2d) 168 (S.C.J.).
[29]   [2002] O.J. No. 665, 58 O.R. (3d) 299 (S.C.J.).
[30]   Man. Reg. 176/2000. See Appendix II.
[31]   Appendix I, s. 4(1).

name and the date of the contract. The supplier may provide the contract to the consumer by e-mail, fax, or surface mail, provided the respective address or number has been supplied by the consumer for the provision of information related to the contract; by active transmission to the consumer in a manner that ensures that the consumer is able to retain the copy; or by any other manner, provided the supplier can prove that the consumer received the copy.[32]

C. Contract Formation

An Internet consumer sales contract is fundamentally a specialized category of electronic contract. Consequently, the rules and outstanding questions that are highlighted in Chapter 1 will equally apply to online consumer contracts unless online consumer protection legislation adds to this understanding. The *Template* does not, except in one respect, address the mechanics of online contract formation, which means that a particular jurisdiction's electronic commerce legislation would be the primary source of law in determining contract formation issues.

The *Template* does require that a consumer be given an express opportunity to accept or decline the online contract and to correct errors immediately before entering into the agreement.[33] Such an opportunity is in practice usually manifested by requiring the consumer to review the terms of the agreement and specifically indicating that a subsequent electronic action, such as clicking an "I agree" icon, concludes the agreement. A similar requirement is also found in the *Uniform Electronic Commerce Act* (*"UECA"*)[34] and most provincial electronic commerce legislation based on that model law. Section 22 of the *UECA* deals with interactions between natural persons and electronic agents (*i.e.*, computer programs that respond electronically without human review) and stipulates that an electronic agent must provide the natural person with the opportunity to prevent or correct an error.[35] Although most online

---

[32] *Ibid.*, s. 4(3).

[33] *Ibid.*, s. 3(1)(b).

[34] Uniform Law Conference of Canada, online: <http://www.ulcc.ca/en/us/index.cfm?sec=1&sub=1u1>.

[35] *Ibid.*, s. 22:

An electronic document made by a natural person with the electronic agent of another person has no legal effect and is not enforceable if the natural person made a material error in the document and

(*a*) the electronic agent did not provide the natural person with an opportunity to prevent or correct the error;

consumer transactions will involve interactions with electronic agents, the *Template* provision is not confined to electronic agents and could, for example, also apply to contracts formed by e-mail.

D.   Cancellation

The issue of whether online consumers should be entitled to a "cooling-off" period, giving them the right to cancel a contract within a certain timeframe consistent with legislation governing direct selling, has often arisen in discussions about online consumer protection.[36] The *Template* does not provide for a cooling off period *per se*, but does allow consumers to cancel an online agreement in specific circumstances that relate to the supplier's failure to abide by the *Template*'s requirements.

According to the *Template,* a consumer may cancel an Internet sales contract in the following circumstances:[37]

- at any time from the date the contract is entered into until seven days after the consumer receives a copy of the contract if the supplier does not disclose to the consumer the information described in Section B, above, or the supplier does not provide to the consumer an express opportunity to accept or decline the contract or to correct errors immediately before entering into it;
- within 30 days from the date the contract is entered into if the supplier does not provide the consumer with a copy of the contract;
- at any time before delivery of the goods or the commencement of the services under the contract if, in the case of goods, the supplier does not deliver the goods within 30 days from the delivery date specified in the contract or an amended delivery date agreed on by the consumer and the supplier, either in writing or in electronic form, or in the case of services, the supplier does not begin the services within 30 days from the commencement date specified in

---

(*b*)   the natural person notifies the other person of the error as soon as practicable after the natural person learns of the error and indicates that he or she made an error in the electronic document;

(*c*)   the natural person takes reasonable steps, including steps that conform to the other person's instructions to return the consideration received, if any, as a result of the error or, if instructed to do so, to destroy the consideration; and

(*d*)   the natural person has not used or received any material benefit or value from the consideration, if any, received from the other person.

[36]   See, for example, the 1998 Report to the Office of Consumer Affairs, Industry Canada, online: <http://www.chlc.ca/en/cls/index.cfm?sec=4&sub=4j>.

[37]   Appendix I, s. 5.

the contract or an amended commencement date agreed on by the consumer and the supplier, either in writing or in electronic form;

• at any time before the delivery of the goods or the commencement of the services under the contract if the delivery date or commencement date is not specified and the supplier does not deliver the goods or begin the services within 30 days from the date the contract is entered into.

A consumer who elects to provide a notice of cancellation may express his or her intention in any way, and the notice may be delivered to the supplier by any means. Where the notice of cancellation is given other than by personal service, the notice of cancellation is deemed to be given when sent.[38] A cancellation of an Internet sales contract effectively operates to cancel the contract and any security given in respect of the contract, as if they had never existed.[39] The *Template* also anticipates situations where, despite the fact that a consumer has a right to cancel an Internet sales contract, it might be inequitable to do so. In such cases, a court of the relevant jurisdiction can make any order it considers appropriate.[40]

After cancellation, the *Template* places additional requirements on both the consumer and the supplier. For example, the supplier must, within 15 days from the date of cancellation, refund to the consumer all consideration paid by the consumer under the contract.[41] A consumer must, within 15 days from the date of cancellation or delivery of the goods, whichever is later, return the goods to the supplier unused and in the same condition in which they were delivered if the consumer elects to exercise the right to cancel the contract.[42] The supplier must accept a return of goods by a consumer in these circumstances, and is responsible for the reasonable cost of returning them.[43] Any breach of the consumer's obligations to return the goods is actionable by the supplier as a breach of statutory duty.[44]

It should be noted again that in those jurisdictions that have passed legislation that reflect the *Template,* a consumer's right of cancellation may vary from the time periods or even the circumstances specified in the

---

[38] *Ibid.*, s. 7.
[39] *Ibid.*, s. 8(1); s. 8(2)(c).
[40] *Ibid.*, s. 6.
[41] *Ibid.*, s. 9(1).
[42] *Ibid.*, s. 9(1), (2).
[43] *Ibid.*, s. 9(4), (5).
[44] *Ibid.*, s. 9(7).

Template. The Concordance in Appendix II herein should be consulted for particulars.

Finally, it is possible that in some jurisdictions, Internet sales may be subject to legislation regulating direct sellers.[45] In those circumstances, the "cooling-off" period that applies to direct selling could arguably also apply to Internet sales contracts.

E.   Reversal of Credit Card Charges

As indicated above, a supplier is required to refund to the consumer all consideration that has been paid pursuant to the contract upon cancellation by the consumer. However, the *Template* recognizes the role of credit card issuers as intermediaries in most online transactions, and provides a mechanism for consumers to receive a reversal of credit card charges. Such a mechanism is important in online transactions, as the supplier will likely be in a distant jurisdiction that would make it difficult for the consumer to pursue a claim.

The *Template* allows a consumer who has charged to a credit card account all or any part of the consideration payable under an Internet sales contract to *request* the credit card issuer to cancel or reverse the credit card charge and any associated interest or other charges where the consumer has cancelled the contract in circumstances when he or she is entitled to do so, and the supplier has not refunded all of the consideration within the stipulated 15-day period.[46]

Upon receipt of the request, the credit card issuer must acknowledge its receipt within 30 days of receiving it, and if the request contains the specified information required to identify the transaction (credit card number, date of transaction, description of the goods or services, *etc.*) the credit card issuer *must* cancel or reverse the credit card charge and any associated interest or other charges within two complete billing cycles of the credit card issuer or 90 days, whichever first occurs.[47] A contravention

---

[45] "Direct selling" legislation usually targets sales or solicitations for future delivery of goods or services where contact is made outside of a retail outlet. In some jurisdictions, the legislation regulating direct sales clearly exempts Internet sales (for example, the British Columbia *Consumer Protection Act*, R.S.B.C. 1996, c. 69, s. 1(1), provides that a "direct sale" does not include a contract where the sale is made by telecommunications or does not involve face-to-face contact with the intended purchaser). In jurisdictions that do not clearly exempt telecommunications, the issue remains outstanding.

[46] Appendix I, s. 11.

[47] *Ibid.*

of the credit card issuer's duties under the *Template* would constitute an offence.[48]

Of the provincial jurisdictions that have enacted Internet-specific consumer protection legislation, most have adopted the credit card charge-back requirements of the *Template*. However, Ontario has elected to give credit card issuers a discretionary right to refuse reversal if, after an investigation has been conducted, the issuer is of the opinion that the consumer is not entitled to cancel the agreement or demand a refund.[49] Such an approach is consistent with the American *Fair Credit Billing Act*,[50] but deviates from the requirements of the *Template*. With respect to online transactions, the difference may not actually have much of an effect, as most credit card issuers have policies that allow for a disputed charge to be charged back to the vendor in "card not present" transactions (where proof of authorization or a signature is not provided). Some issuers even promise zero liability to customers who are victims of credit card fraud over the Internet. However, the circumstances in which reversals will be granted and the process involved will be dictated by the credit card agreement, whereas the *Template* provides a standard legal course of action aimed at providing a relatively prompt recourse for the consumer, and a punishable offence when the rules are contravened.[51]

III. JURISDICTION

The strongest consumer protection legislation possible will not help a consumer if the vendor is not subject to the law's jurisdiction. This is, of course, a significant issue with respect to online consumer transactions, where the likelihood is great that the parties reside in different countries, or different parts of the same country, like Canada, with different consumer protection legislation regimes. Consumers would obviously prefer to take action in their home jurisdictions, especially when their domestic consumer protection laws stipulate, as they generally do in Canada, that they will apply regardless of any stipulation to the contrary in the contract with the seller.

---

[48] *Ibid.*, s. 12.

[49] *Consumer Protection Act, 2002,* S.O. 2002, c. 30, Sch. A., s. 99.

[50] 15 U.S.C. 1601.

[51] It should be noted that with respect to unauthorized use of lost or stolen credit cards, federal and provincial legislation generally limits the liability of the cardholder to $50. See, for example, the *Cost of Borrowing (Banks) Regulations,* SOR/2001-101, s. 12, issued under the authority of the federal *Bank Act,* S.C. 1991, c. 46.

From a seller's perspective, selling to consumers over the Internet could potentially subject the seller to countless legal consequences, and thus the seller may understandably wish to limit liability, or at least limit the jurisdiction of the contract, by inserting forum selection and choice of law clauses into agreements. Courts in Canada have generally been inclined to uphold such clauses where there is no legislative requirement to treat them as void.[52]

The *Template* essentially avoids the issue of jurisdiction, leaving it to the particular jurisdiction that adopts it to determine the scope of the law. The various alternatives from a consumer protection perspective would include reliance on Canadian jurisprudence in relation to what constitutes a "real and substantial connection" to the jurisdiction, or the application of a "jurisdiction of destination approach", or some variant thereof, in which the law and forum of the purchaser would apply to the transaction.

Most jurisdictions that are serious about online consumer protection have implemented a "jurisdiction of destination" approach to online consumer protection. In other words, sellers who do business with individuals within a given jurisdiction will be subjecting themselves to the consumer protection regime of that jurisdiction. The European Union's Brussels Regulation[53] has adopted a variation of this model, which allows a consumer to sue a seller in the consumer's state of domicile if the seller "targets" the consumer's jurisdiction by pursuing commercial activities. With respect to the Internet, accessibility of the seller's Web site within the jurisdiction is not sufficient by itself to indicate that the seller is doing business within the jurisdiction, although solicitation via the Web site could raise that implication.[54]

Of the provinces that have adopted the provisions of the *Template*, Alberta provides the clearest guidance on the issue of the application of its law to consumer agreements. Alberta's *Internet Sales Contract Regulation*[55] states that its provisions apply to Internet sales contracts in which the supplier or consumer is resident in Alberta, and in which the offer or acceptance is made in or sent from Alberta.[56] Alberta's online consumers consequently have some assurance that they will be covered by that province's online consumer protection rules. In other provinces, such

---

[52]   See the discussion in Chapter 1.

[53]   Council Regulation (EC) No. 44/2001.

[54]   The Brussels Regulation: The Council and Commission's Joint Statement on Articles 15 and 68, available online: <http://www.dti.gov.uk/consumers/consumer-support/resolving-disputes/jurisdiction/brussels/index.html>.

[55]   Alta. Reg. 81/2001.

[56]   *Ibid.*, s. 2.

as Nova Scotia, where the legislation is silent as to jurisdiction, it may be necessary to establish that the contract has a "real and substantial" connection to the province.

A recent proposal contained in a consultation paper on jurisdiction in cross-border business-to-consumer transactions, prepared by the Consumer Measures Committee and the Uniform Law Conference of Canada, would allow parties to a consumer contract to agree which law will apply to the contract, but such agreement would not deprive a consumer of the protection to which the consumer is entitled under his or her home jurisdiction if certain circumstances are present:[57]

- the consumer contract resulted from a solicitation of business in the consumer's jurisdiction by or on behalf of the vendor and the consumer took all the necessary steps for the formation of the consumer contract in the consumer's jurisdiction; or
- the consumer's order was received by the vendor in the consumer's jurisdiction; or
- the consumer was induced by the vendor to travel to a foreign jurisdiction for the purpose of forming the contract and the consumer's travel was assisted by the vendor.

If there is no agreement as to the applicable law in a consumer contract, the law of the consumer's jurisdiction would apply provided that at least one of the conditions set out above is met. The proposal leaves open the possibility that a consumer contract formed in the consumer's jurisdiction could have the laws of the seller's jurisdiction applied to it if it can be demonstrated that the seller took reasonable steps to avoid concluding contracts within the consumer's jurisdiction.

The proposal gives the consumer the option of bringing proceedings against the vendor either in the courts of the consumer's jurisdiction or in the courts of the vendor's jurisdiction if:

- the consumer contract resulted from a solicitation of business in the consumer's jurisdiction by or on behalf of the vendor and the consumer took all the necessary steps for the formation of the consumer contract in the consumer's jurisdiction; or
- the consumer's order was received by the vendor in the consumer's jurisdiction, or the consumer was induced by the vendor to travel to a foreign jurisdiction for the purpose of forming the contract and the consumer's travel was assisted by the vendor.

---

[57] Available from Industry Canada online: <http://strategis.ic.gc.ca/epic/internet/inoca-bc.nsf/ vwapj/ca01862e.pdf/$FILE/ca01862e.pdf>.

A vendor would be able to bring proceedings against the consumer only in the courts of the consumer's jurisdiction.

Draft legislation reflecting these proposals has been released by the Uniform Law Conference of Canada.[58] As of this writing, the proposals are still being reviewed.

IV. THE *COMPETITION ACT*[59]

Although the focus of this chapter has been consumer protection legislation that concentrates on Internet communications, it was stated earlier that general consumer protection legislation would also apply to online transactions. Accordingly, some discussion of the federal *Competition Act* is warranted in this chapter, as several of its provisions have potential application to specific problems that arise in the context of online buying and selling.

The application of provisions of the *Competition Act* to novel online consumer protection issues such as "phishing" and "spyware" is discussed in Chapters 3 and 4. But the Act also contains provisions that would apply to concerns that arise in the course of online contracting and advertising.

First, it is an offence under the Act for a person to knowingly or recklessly make a representation to the public that is false or misleading in a material respect for the purpose of promoting, directly or indirectly, the supply or use of a product, or any business interest, *by any means whatever.*[60] The Competition Bureau has issued an Information Bulletin[61] on the application of the *Competition Act* to representations made on the Internet, which clearly states:

> The Act applies equally to false or misleading representations regardless of the medium used. The same basic rules that govern truthfulness in traditional advertising and marketing practices apply to on-line representations and on-line marketing practices. The relevant provisions of the Act address the substance of a representation rather than the means by which it is made.[62]

Any person who makes a false or misleading representation to the public is guilty of an offence and liable on conviction on indictment, to a

---

[58] Online: <http://chlc.ca/en/us/unit_jur_choice_law_consumer_contracts_en.pdf>.
[59] R.S.C. 1985, c. C-34.
[60] *Ibid.*, s. 52(1).
[61] Online: <http://www.competitionbureau.gc.ca/PDFS/ct02500e.pdf> (hereinafter *Bulletin*).
[62] *Ibid.*, at 2.

fine in the discretion of the court or to imprisonment for a term not exceeding five years or to both, or on summary conviction, to a fine not exceeding $200,000 or to imprisonment for a term not exceeding one year, or to both.[63]

The Act stipulates that the misrepresentation must generally be made to the public by the person who causes the representation to be expressed.[64] Where the representation is transmitted from outside Canada, it is deemed to be made to the public by the person who imports it into Canada.[65] Would Internet service providers and other intermediaries therefore be deemed to make representations? In the view of the Competition Bureau, the nature and degree of control that a person exercises over the content of a representation in the online environment will determine whether the representation has been caused by that person.[66] The Bureau's *Bulletin* indicates that in most circumstances, intermediaries such as Internet service providers and web designers would not normally be the persons who caused the representation, although that possibility is not foreclosed in circumstances where such intermediaries have control over content.[67] (It should be noted that this interpretation applies only in respect of the *Competition Act* and does not necessarily reflect an approach that will be taken pursuant to other laws.)

As we have seen, jurisdictional issues are particularly problematic with respect to online interactions. The *Bulletin* indicates that "the Bureau will assert Canadian jurisdiction over foreign entities to the fullest extent authorized by law whenever necessary to protect the Canadian market from misleading representations".[68] This rather vague statement does not indicate the circumstances in which those making representations from outside Canada could be held liable under the Act. The only clear statement on jurisdiction states that persons who make online representations from Canada that are accessible in Canada are required to comply with the Act.[69]

---

[63] *Competition Act*, R.S.C. 1985, c. C-34, s. 52(5).

[64] *Ibid.*, s. 52(2).

[65] *Ibid.*, s. 52(2.1).

[66] Online: <http://www.competitionbureau.gc.ca/PDFS/ct02500e.pdf>, at 6.

[67] *Ibid.* The Bureau indicates that it will focus its enforcement efforts primarily on businesses that are responsible for content or have a degree of control over that content, rather than on businesses operating as a conduit, which is analogous to a traditional disseminator or distributor of the content (at 7).

[68] *Ibid.*, at 12.

[69] *Ibid.*

The question of how far a state's regulatory jurisdiction should extend is difficult and complicated by constitutional issues.[70] Canadian courts generally determine whether there is a "real and substantial connection" between the offence and Canada. That is, if a significant portion of the activities constituting the offence take place in Canada, the offence would be subject to the jurisdiction of Canadian courts.[71]

Related to the prohibition on misleading representations, Part VII.I of the *Competition Act* sets up an administrative procedure dealing with deceptive marketing. Making certain misleading representations relating to issues such as product warranties, prices, or performance constitutes "reviewable conduct" that can result in administrative sanctions or orders.[72] Representations transmitted or made available in any other manner to a member of the public are captured, and the Competition Bureau has employed these "reviewable conduct" provisions to shut down misleading Web businesses.[73]

Part VII.I provides a defence to any person who merely disseminates or distributes a misleading representation.[74] According to the *Bulletin,* the defence "is available to any person who does not have decision-making authority or control over the content".[75] Again, the Bureau indicates that it will focus its enforcement efforts primarily on businesses which are responsible for content or have a degree of control over that content, rather than the carrier of the content.[76]

The deceptive notice of winning a prize provision of the *Competition Act* expressly prohibits sending electronic mail to promote a business interest that, without giving adequate disclosure, gives the general impression that the recipient has won, will win, or will on doing a

---

[70] See, for example, the controversial issue of whether France's anti-racism laws could be enforced against an Internet service provider in the United States. The U.S. District Court in California held that it could not enforce such a foreign Order that violated the U.S.'s First Amendment: *Yahoo! Inc. v. La Ligue Contre le Racisme et L'Antisemitisme*, 169 F. Supp. 2d 1181 (N.D. Cal. 2001).

[71] See, for example, *R. v. Libman*, [1985] S.C.J. No. 56, [1985] 2 S.C.R. 178.

[72] R.S.C. 1985, c. C-34, s. 74.01.

[73] *Ibid.*, s. 74.03. For example, in February 2006 the Competition Bureau reached a settlement with respect to two Internet scams that promoted resume distribution services. The Web sites misrepresented the effectiveness of the services provided and provided phoney customer testimonials. The offenders were required to pay an administrative penalty of $100,000, admit to having committed reviewable conduct under the *Competition Act,* and discontinue the offending conduct on the Web sites. See February 22, 2006 press release, "Competition Bureau shuts down Internet-based job scams", online: <http://www.competitionbureau.gc.ca>.

[74] *Ibid.*, s. 74.07.

[75] Online: <http://www.competitionbureau.gc.ca/PDFS/ct02500e.pdf>, at 7.

[76] *Ibid.*

particular act win, a prize, if the recipient is asked or given the option to pay money, incur a cost or do anything that will incur a cost.[77] This provision could be useful in targeting many types of spam. Any person who contravenes this provision is guilty of an offence and liable to significant penalties or imprisonment.[78] Moreover, any officer or director of the corporation who is in a position to direct or influence the policies of the corporation may also be liable to the punishment provided for the offence,[79] and the court is entitled in sentencing to consider issues such as the manner in which information is conveyed, such as the use of abusive tactics, and the amount of the proceeds realized from the commission of the offence.[80]

The *Bulletin* clearly states that improper placement of disclaimers on Web sites could amount to representations that are misleading and in violation of the *Competition Act.* Disclaimers should be placed prominently and conspicuously, and should appear whenever possible on the same screen and close to the representation to which it relates.[81] The *Bulletin* also provides the Bureau's views on scrolling (sellers must ensure that the disclaimer is viewable by consumers no matter what hardware or software they use) and hyperlinks and "pop-ups" (which the Bureau feels can be an effective means of providing disclaimers, provided they are clear and the consumer is not likely to be misled).[82] The *Bulletin* also suggests that vendors make clicking through a disclaimer compulsory, and stipulates that in some circumstances, it is not sufficient that the disclaimer appear only on the order page.[83]

Finally, the *Bulletin* interprets the term "interactive telephone communications" in relation to deceptive telemarketing[84] to mean live voice communications, but indicates that as Internet services evolve, this interpretation will be re-evaluated.[85]

It should be noted that provincial jurisdictions have also passed unfair trade practices legislation that will regulate false, misleading, or deceptive representations within their respective jurisdictions.[86] False or

---

[77] R.S.C. 1985, c. C-34, s. 53(1).
[78] *Ibid.*, s. 53(6).
[79] *Ibid.*, s. 53(5).
[80] *Ibid.*, s. 53(7).
[81] Online: <http://www.competitionbureau.gc.ca/PDFS/ct02500e.pdf>, at 8.
[82] *Ibid.*
[83] *Ibid.*, at 10.
[84] R.S.C. 1985, c. C-34, s. 52.1.
[85] Online: <http://www.competitionbureau.gc.ca/PDFS/ct02500e.pdf>, at 12.
[86] For example, Ontario's *Consumer Protection Act, 2002,* S.O. 2002, c. 30, Sch. A incorporates all of the provisions previously contained in the *Business Practices Act.*

misleading advertising relating to various specific products, which would include making such representations over the Internet, are also prohibited by certain federal statutes.[87]

---

[87] For example, the *Precious Metals Marking Act*, R.S.C. 1985, c. P-19.

Appendix I

INTERNET SALES CONTRACT HARMONIZATION TEMPLATE

Definitions[1]

1 In this **[indicate Act or Regulation]**,

(a) "consumer" means **[generally, a consumer is an individual who receives or has the right to receive goods or services from a supplier as a result of a purchase, lease or other arrangement]**;[2]

(b) "consumer transaction" means the supply of goods or services by a supplier to a consumer as a result of a purchase, lease or other arrangement;

(c) "goods" means **[generally, goods are any personal property that is used primarily for personal, family or household purposes]**;[3]

(d) "internet" means the decentralized global network connecting networks of computers and similar devices to each other for the electronic exchange of information using standardized communication protocols;[4]

(e) "internet sales contract" means a consumer transaction formed by text-based internet communications;

(f) "services" means **[generally, services are any services offered or provided primarily for personal, family or household purposes]**;[5]

(g) "supplier" means **[generally, a supplier is a person who in the course of the person's business provides goods or services to consumers]**.[6]

---

[1] For consistency with existing legislation, each jurisdiction will need to determine what definitions are necessary.

[2] See, for example, s. 1(1)(b) of Alberta's *Fair Trading Act*, R.S.A. 2000, c. F-2.

[3] See, for example, s. 1(1)(e) of Alberta's *Fair Trading Act*, R.S.A. 2000, c. F-2.

[4] See, for example, s. 127 of Manitoba's *Consumer Protection Act*, C.C.S.M. c. C200.

[5] See, for example, s. 1(1)(k) of Alberta's *Fair Trading Act*, R.S.A. 2000, c. F-2.

[6] See, for example, s. 1(1)(l) of Alberta's *Fair Trading Act*, R.S.A. 2000, c. F-2.

Application

2 [Each jurisdiction will need to determine the scope of the template, including determining whether certain classes of businesses[7] or certain types of goods and services, or both, should be excluded from all or some of the provisions.]

Disclosure of information

3(1) A supplier must do the following before a consumer enters into an internet sales contract:

(a) disclose to the consumer the following information:

(i) the supplier's name and, if different, the name under which the supplier carries on business;

(ii) the supplier's business address and, if different, the supplier's mailing address;

(iii) the supplier's telephone number and, if available, the supplier's e-mail address and facsimile number;

(iv) a fair and accurate description of the goods or services being sold to the consumer, including any relevant technical or system specifications;

(v) an itemized list of the price of the goods or services being sold to the consumer and any associated costs payable by the consumer, including taxes and shipping charges;

(vi) a description of any additional charges that may apply to the contract, such as customs duties and brokerage fees, whose amounts cannot reasonably be determined by the supplier;

(vii) the total amount of the contract or, where the goods or services are being purchased over an indefinite period, the amount of the periodic payments under the contract;

(viii) the currency in which amounts owing under the contract are payable;

---

[7]   There may be several reasons why the proposals should not apply to a particular class of business. For instance, a consumer's rights and remedies in respect of a particular transaction may be addressed in another Act or regulation.

(ix) the terms, conditions and method of payment;

(x) the date when the goods are to be delivered or the services are to begin;

(xi) the supplier's delivery arrangements, including the identity of the shipper, the mode of transportation and the place of delivery;

(xii) the supplier's cancellation, return, exchange and refund policies, if any;

(xiii) any other restrictions, limitations or conditions of purchase that may apply;

(b) provide the consumer with an express opportunity to accept or decline the contract and to correct errors[8] immediately before entering into it.

(2) For the purposes of subsection (1), a supplier is considered to have disclosed to the consumer the information described in subsection (1)(a) if the information is

(a) prominently displayed in a clear and comprehensible manner, and

(b) made accessible in a manner that ensures that
      (i) the consumer has accessed the information, and
      (ii) the consumer is able to retain and print the information.

Copy of internet sales contract

4(1) A supplier must provide a consumer who enters into an internet sales contract with a copy of the contract in writing or electronic form within 15 days after the contract is entered into.

(2) The copy of the internet sales contract under subsection (1) must include

(a) the information described in section 3(1)(a),

(b) the consumer's name, and

(c) the date the contract was entered into.

---

[8] This reflects the *Uniform Electronic Commerce Act*'s provision on error correction.

(3) For the purposes of subsection (1), a supplier is considered to have provided the consumer with a copy of the internet sales contract if the copy is

(a) sent by e-mail to the e-mail address provided by the consumer to the supplier for the provision of information related to the contract,

(b) sent by facsimile to the facsimile number provided by the consumer to the supplier for the provision of information related to the contract,

(c) mailed or delivered to an address provided by the consumer to the supplier for the provision of information related to the contract,

(d) actively transmitted to the consumer in a manner that ensures that the consumer is able to retain the copy, or

(e) provided to the consumer in any other manner by which the supplier can prove that the consumer has received the copy.

Cancellation of internet sales contract

5(1) A consumer may cancel an internet sales contract in the following circumstances:

(a) at any time from the date the contract is entered into until 7 days after the consumer receives a copy of the contract if
> (i) the supplier does not disclose to the consumer the information described in section 3(1)(a), or
> (ii) the supplier does not provide to the consumer an express opportunity to accept or decline the contract or to correct errors immediately before entering into it;

(b) within 30 days from the date the contract is entered into if the supplier does not provide the consumer with a copy of the contract pursuant to section 4.

(2) In addition to the cancellation rights under subsection (1), a consumer may cancel an internet sales contract at any time before delivery of the goods or the commencement of the services under the contract if

(a) in the case of goods, the supplier does not deliver the goods within 30 days from the delivery date specified in the contract or an amended delivery date agreed on by the consumer and the supplier, either in writing or in electronic form, or

(b) in the case of services, the supplier does not begin the services within 30 days from the commencement date specified in the contract or an amended commencement date agreed on by the consumer and the supplier, either in writing or in electronic form.

(3) If the delivery date or commencement date is not specified in the internet sales contract, a consumer may cancel the contract at any time before the delivery of the goods or the commencement of the services under the contract if the supplier does not deliver the goods or begin the services within 30 days from the date the contract is entered into.

(4) For the purposes of subsections (2) and (3),

(a) a supplier is considered to have delivered the goods under an internet sales contract if
> (i) delivery was attempted but was refused by the consumer at the time that delivery was attempted, or
> (ii) delivery was attempted but not made because no person was available to accept delivery for the consumer on the day for which reasonable notice was given to the consumer that the goods were available to be delivered;

(b) a supplier is considered to have begun the services under an internet sales contract if
> (i) commencement was attempted but was refused by the consumer at the time that commencement was attempted, or
> (ii) commencement was attempted but did not occur because no person was available to enable the services to begin on the day for which reasonable notice was given to the consumer that the services were available to begin.

Court may provide relief against cancellation

6 If in the opinion of the [**indicate level of court**] it would be inequitable for an internet sales contract to be cancelled under section 5, the court may make any order it considers appropriate.[9]

Notice of cancellation

7(1) An internet sales contract is cancelled under section 5 on the giving of a notice of cancellation in accordance with this section.

---

[9] Jurisdictions may want to provide a list of examples of inequitable situations for illustrative purposes.

(2) A notice of cancellation may be expressed in any way as long as it indicates the intention of the consumer to cancel the internet sales contract.

(3) The notice of cancellation may be given to the supplier by any means, including, but not limited to, personal service, registered mail, telephone, courier, facsimile and e-mail.

(4) Where the notice of cancellation is given other than by personal service, the notice of cancellation is deemed to be given when sent.

Effect of cancellation

8(1) A cancellation of an internet sales contract under section 5 operates to cancel the contract as if the contract had never existed.

(2) A cancellation of an internet sales contract under section 5 also operates to cancel

(a) any related consumer transaction,

(b) any guarantee given in respect of consideration payable under the contract, and

(c) any security given by the consumer or a guarantor in respect of consideration payable under the contract, as if the contract had never existed.

(3) Where credit is extended or arranged by the supplier, the credit contract is conditional on the internet sales contract whether or not the credit contract is a part of or attached to the internet sales contract, and if the internet sales contract is cancelled, that cancellation has the effect of cancelling the credit contract as if the internet sales contract had never existed.

Responsibilities on cancellation

9(1) If an internet sales contract is cancelled under section 5, the supplier must, within 15 days from the date of cancellation, refund to the consumer all consideration paid by the consumer under the contract and any related consumer transaction, whether paid to the supplier or another person.

(2) If goods are delivered to a consumer under an internet sales contract that is cancelled under section 5, the consumer must, within 15 days from the date of cancellation or delivery of the goods, whichever is later, return the goods to the supplier unused and in the same condition in which they were delivered.

(3) The consumer may return the goods under subsection (2) by any method that provides the consumer with confirmation of delivery to the supplier.

(4) The supplier must accept a return of goods by a consumer under subsection (2).

(5) The supplier is responsible for the reasonable cost of returning goods under subsection (2).

(6) Goods that are returned by the consumer under subsection (2) otherwise than by personal delivery are deemed for the purposes of that subsection to have been returned when sent by the consumer to the supplier.

(7) Any breach of the consumer's obligations under this section is actionable by the supplier as a breach of statutory duty.

Recovery of refund

10 If a consumer has cancelled an internet sales contract under section 5 and the supplier has not refunded all of the consideration within the 15-day period referred to in section 9(1), the consumer may recover the consideration from the supplier as an action in debt.

Consumer's recourse re credit card charges

11(1) A consumer who has charged to a credit card account all or any part of the consideration payable under an internet sales contract or related consumer transaction may request the credit card issuer to cancel or reverse the credit card charge and any associated interest or other charges where the consumer has cancelled the contract under section 5 and the supplier has not refunded all of the consideration within the 15-day period referred to in section 9(1).

(2) A request under subsection (1) must be in writing or electronic form and contain the following information:

(a) the consumer's name;

(b) the consumer's credit card number;

(c) the expiry date of the consumer's credit card;

(d) the supplier's name;

(e) the date the internet sales contract was entered into;

(f) the dollar amount of consideration charged to the credit card account in respect of the internet sales contract and any related consumer transaction;

(g) a description of the goods or services sufficient to identify them;

(h) the reason for cancellation of the internet sales contract under section 5;

(i) the date and method of cancellation of the internet sales contract.

(3) The credit card issuer must

(a) acknowledge the consumer's request within 30 days of receiving it, and

(b) if the request meets the requirements of subsection (2), cancel or reverse the credit card charge and any associated interest or other charges within 2 complete billing cycles of the credit card issuer or 90 days, whichever first occurs.

(4) A request under subsection (1) may be given to the credit card issuer by any means, including, but not limited to, personal service, registered mail, courier, facsimile and e-mail.
(5) Where the request is given other than by personal service, the request is deemed to be given when sent.

Offence

12 A contravention of section 9(1) or 11(3) is an offence for the purposes of [**indicate section of relevant Act**].

Appendix II

INTERNET SALES CONTRACT HARMONIZATION TEMPLATE CONCORDANCE WITH PROVINCIAL LEGISLATION

LEGISLATION (SEE APPENDIX I)

Internet Sales Contract Harmonization Template, Industry Canada (<http://strategis.ic.gc.ca/epic/internet/inoca-bc.nsf/en/ca01642e.html>) [*Template*]

Alberta

Fair Trading Act, R.S.A. 2000, c. F-2. [AFTA]

Internet Sales Contract Regulation, Alta. Reg. 81/2001. [AISCR]

British Columbia

Business Practices and Consumer Protection Act, S.B.C. 2004, c. 2. [BPCPA]

Consumer Contracts Regulations, B.C. Reg. 272/2004.

Manitoba

Consumer Protection Act, C.C.S.M, c. C200. [MCPA]

Internet Agreements Regulation, Man. Reg. 176/2000. [IAR]

Nova Scotia

Consumer Protection Act, R.S.N.S 1989, c. 92. [NSCPA]

Internet Sales Contract Regulations, N.S. Reg. 91/2002. [NSISCR]

Ontario

Consumer Protection Act, 2002, S.O. 2002, c. 30, Sch. A. [OCPA]

O. Reg. 17/05 [OCPA Regs.]

DEFINITIONS

"Consumer"

> **Sec. 1 In this [indicate Act or Regulation],**
>
> > **(a) "consumer" means [generally, a consumer is an individual who receives or has the right to receive goods or services from a supplier as a result of a purchase, lease or other arrangement];**

Provincial Legislation

Alberta—AFTA, s. 1(1) In this Act …

(b) "consumer" means, subject to the regulations under subsection (2), an individual who

> (i)   receives or has the right to receive goods or services from a supplier as a result of a purchase, lease, gift, contest or other arrangement, but does not include an individual who intends to sell the goods after receiving them,
>
> (ii)   has a legal obligation to compensate a supplier for goods that have been or are to be supplied to another individual and the other individual does not intend to sell the goods after receiving them, or
>
> (iii) has a legal obligation to compensate a supplier for services that have been or are to be supplied to another individual;

British Columbia—BPCPA, s. 1(1) In this Act …

"consumer" means an individual, whether in British Columbia or not, who participates in a consumer transaction, but does not include a guarantor;

Manitoba—the MCPA uses the term "buyer"; MCPA—s. 1(1), In this Act …

"buyer" includes a hirer on a retail hire-purchase [see variations in Manitoba, below];

Nova Scotia—NSCPA, s. 21V(a)

Ontario—OCPA, s. 1 In this Act …

"consumer" means an individual acting for personal, family or household purposes and does not include a person who is acting for business purposes;

"Consumer Transaction"

Sec. 1. …

(b) "consumer transaction" means the supply of goods or services by a supplier to a consumer as a result of a purchase, lease or other arrangement;

Provincial Legislation

Alberta—AFTA, s. 1(1) In this Act, …

(c) "consumer transaction" means, subject to the regulations under subsection (2) [definitions may be modified],

(i) the supply of goods or services by a supplier to a consumer as a result of a purchase, lease, gift, contest or other arrangement, or

(ii) an agreement between a supplier and a consumer, as a result of a purchase, lease, gift, contest or other arrangement, in which the supplier is to supply goods or services to the consumer or to another consumer specified in the agreement;

British Columbia—s. 1(1) In this Act …

"consumer transaction" means

    (a) a supply of goods or services or real property by a supplier to a consumer for purposes that are primarily personal, family or household, or

    (b) a solicitation, offer, advertisement or promotion by a supplier with respect to a transaction referred to in paragraph (a),

and, [additional part does not apply to distance sales contracts and future performance contracts] ...

Manitoba—see variations below.

Nova Scotia—NSCPA, s. 21V(b)

Ontario—OCPA, s. 1 In this Act ...

"consumer transaction" means any act or instance of conducting business or other dealings with a consumer, including a consumer agreement;

"Goods"

Sec. 1 ...

(c) "goods" means [generally, goods are any personal property that is used primarily for personal, family or household purposes];

Provincial Legislation

Alberta—AFTA, s. 1(1) In this Act ...

    (e) "goods", except in Part 12 [Public Auctions], means, subject to the regulations under subsection (2) [modifying definitions],

        (i)   any personal property that is used or ordinarily used primarily for personal, family or household purposes,

        (ii) a voucher, or

        (iii) a new residential dwelling whether or not the dwelling is affixed to land;

British Columbia—BPCPA s. 1(1) In this Act ...

"goods" means personal property, fixtures and credit, but does not include a security as defined in the *Securities Act* or contracts of insurance under the *Insurance Act*;

Manitoba—see variations, below; MCPA, s. 1(1), In this Act ...

"goods" means chattels personal other than things in action or money, and includes, food products, emblements, industrial growing crops and things attached to or forming part of the land which are agreed to be severed before sale or under the contract of sale, and chattels which are to be affixed to land upon or after delivery thereof

Nova Scotia—NSCPA, s. 2 In this Act ...

    (f) "goods" includes tokens, coupons or other documents or things issued or sold by a seller to a buyer that are exchangeable or redeemable for goods or services;

Ontario—OCPA, s. 1 In this Act, ...

"goods" means any type of property;

"Internet"

Sec. 1 ...

    (d) "internet" means the decentralized global network connecting networks of computers and similar devices to each other for the electronic exchange of information using standardized communication protocols;

Provincial Legislation

Alberta—AISCR, s. 1(c)

British Columbia—see variations below.

Manitoba—MCPA, s. 127

Nova Scotia—NSCPA, s. 21V(c)

Ontario—OCPA, s. 20(1)

"Internet Sales Contract"

Sec. 1 ...

(e) "internet sales contract" means a consumer transaction formed by text-based internet communications;

Provincial Legislation

Alberta—AISCR, s. 1 In this Regulation ...

> (d) "internet sales contract" means a consumer transaction that is a contract in which
>
> > (i) the consideration for the goods or services exceeds $50, and
> >
> > (ii) the contract is formed by text-based Internet communications.

British Columbia—see variations below.

Manitoba—see variations below; MCPA, s. 128

> This Part [XVI, Internet Agreements] applies to retail sale or retail hire-purchase agreements formed by Internet communications.

Nova Scotia—NSCPA, s. 21V(d)

Ontario—Ontario uses the term "internet agreement" instead of "internet sales contract"; OCPA, s. 20

> "internet agreement" means a consumer agreement formed by text-based internet communications;
>
> s. 1 "consumer agreement" means an agreement between a supplier and a consumer in which the supplier agrees to supply goods or services for payment;

"Services"

Sec. 1 ...

    (f) "services" means [generally, services are any services offered or provided primarily for personal, family or household purposes];

Provincial Legislation

Alberta—AFTA, s. 1(1) In this Act, ...

    (k) "services" means, subject to the regulations under subsection (2), any service offered or provided primarily for personal, family or household purposes, including

        (i) a service offered or provided that involves the addition to or maintenance, repair or alteration of goods or any residential dwelling,

        (ii) a membership in any club or organization if the club or organization is a business formed to make a profit for its owners,

        (iii) the right to use property under a time share contract;

        (iv) any credit agreement

British Columbia—BPCPA, s. 1(1) In this Act ...

"services" means services, whether or not the services are together with or separate from goods, and includes a membership in a club or organization;

Manitoba—see variations, below. MCPA, s. 1(1) In this Act ...

"services" includes

    (a) work, labour and other personal services;

    (b) privileges with respect to transportation, hotel and restaurant accommodations, education, entertainment, recreation, physical culture, funerals, cemetery accommodations and the like; and

(c) insurance provided by a person other than the insurer;

Nova Scotia—NSCPA, s. 21V(e)

Ontario—OCPA, s. 1, In this Act, ...

"services" means anything other than goods, including any service, right, entitlement or benefit;

"Supplier"

Sec. 1 ...

(g) "supplier" means [generally, a supplier is a person who in the course of the person's business provides goods or services to consumers];

Provincial Legislation

Alberta—AFTA, s. 1(1) In this Act, ...

(l) "supplier" means, subject to the regulations under subsection (2), a person who, in the course of the person's business,

(i) provides goods or services to consumers,

(ii) manufactures, assembles or produces goods,

(iii) promotes the use or purchase of goods or services, or

(iv) receives or is entitled to receive money or other consideration as a result of the provision of goods or services to consumers,

and includes any salesperson, employee, representative or agent of the person.

British Columbia—BPCPA, s. 1(1) In this Act ...

"supplier" means a person, whether in British Columbia or not, who in the course of business participates in a consumer transaction by

(a) supplying goods or services or real property to a consumer, or

(b) soliciting, offering, advertising or promoting with respect to a transaction referred to in paragraph (a) of the definition of "consumer transaction",

whether or not privity of contract exists between that person and the consumer, and includes the successor to, and assignee of, any rights or obligations of that person and, [exception does not apply to distance sales contracts and future performance contracts]

Manitoba—uses the term "seller", MCPA, s. 1(1), In this Act ...

"seller" includes a person who lets goods on hire by a retail hire-purchase [see definition of "retail hire-purchase" above];

Nova Scotia—NSCPA, s. 21V(f)

Ontario—OCPA, s. 1 In this Act ...

"supplier" means a person who is in the business of selling, leasing or trading in goods or services or is otherwise in the business of supplying goods or services, and includes an agent of the supplier and a person who holds themself out to be a supplier or an agent of the supplier;

Provincial Variations

British Columbia

The British Columbia Act does not make reference to the Internet, but "Internet Sales Contracts" as defined in the template would be covered by Part 4 of the BPCPA, "Consumer Contracts," specifically "distance sale contracts" and "future performance contracts".

BPCPA, s. 17 In this Part ...

"distance sales contract" means a contract for the supply of goods or services between a supplier and a consumer that is not entered into in person and, with respect to goods, for which the consumer does not have the opportunity to inspect the goods that are the subject of the contract before the contract is entered into;

...

"future performance contract" means a contract between a supplier and consumer for the supply of goods or services for which the supply or payment in full of the total price payable is not made at the time the contract is made or partly executed, but does not include

  (a) a contract for which the total price payable by the consumer, not including the total cost of credit, is less than a prescribed amount.

  (b) a contract for the supply of goods or services under a credit agreement, as defined in section 57 [definitions], if the goods or services have been supplied, or

  (c) a time share contract;

BPCPA, s. 18

  (1) Subject to subsection (2), if a contract meets the definition of more than one type of contract referred to in this Part [4, Consumer Contracts], all of the applicable provisions in this Part apply to the contract unless a contrary intention appears in this Part.

  (2) If there is a conflict or inconsistency between provisions that apply to a contract, the provision that is most beneficial to the consumer applies to the contract.

Manitoba

Manitoba uses the terms "buyer" and "seller" and not "consumer" and "supplier" as in the *Template*. Additionally, there is no equivalent of "internet sales contract" or "consumer transaction". The legislation generally refers to "retail sale or retail hire-purchase agreements".

The definitions of these terms serves to limit the application of the MCPA in a way similar to the definitions of "goods" and "services".

MCPA, s. 1(1) In this Act …

"retail hire-purchase" of goods means any hiring of goods from a person in the course of his business in which

  (a) the hirer is given an option to purchase the goods; or

  (b) it is agreed that upon compliance with the terms of the contract the hirer will either become the owner of the goods or will be entitled to keep them indefinitely without any further payment;

except

...

(g) a hire-purchase in which the hirer is a corporation; and

(h) a hire-purchase of goods by a hirer who himself intends to use them or uses them for the primary purpose of carrying on a business...

...

"retail sale" of goods or of services or of both means any contract of sale of goods or services or both made by a seller in the course of his business except

(a) any contract of sale of goods which are intended for resale by the buyer in the course of his business unless the buyer intends to resell or re-let the goods or services, or both, in a manner to which Part VII [direct sellers] applies;

...

(d) any contract of sale to a corporation; and

(e) any contract of sale of goods or services intended to be used or used by the purchaser for the primary purpose of carrying on a business, unless the goods or services are intended for resale or re-let in a manner to which Part VII [direct sellers] applies;

Application

2 [Each jurisdiction will need to determine the scope of the template, including determining whether certain classes of businesses or certain types of goods and services, or both, should be excluded from all or some of the provisions.]

Jurisdiction

Alberta—AISCR, s. 2 This Regulation applies to the following Internet sales contracts:

(a) a contract in which the supplier or consumer is a resident of Alberta;

(b) a contract in which the offer or acceptance is made in or is sent from Alberta.

British Columbia

BPCPA, s. 1(1), In this Act ...

"consumer" means an individual, whether in British Columbia or not, who participates in a consumer transaction, but does not include a guarantor;

...

"supplier" means a person, whether in British Columbia or not, who in the course of business participates in a consumer transaction by...

Manitoba—not addressed.

Nova Scotia—not addressed.

Ontario—OCPA, s. 2

(1) Subject to this section, this Act applies in respect of all consumer transactions if the consumer or the person engaging in the transaction with the consumer is located in Ontario when the transaction takes place.

Monetary Limit

Alberta—AISCR, s. 1 ...

(d) "Internet sales contract" means a consumer transaction that is a contract in which

(i) the consideration for the goods or services exceeds $50

(ii) the contract is formed by text-based Internet communications.

British Columbia—for future performance contracts.

BPCPA, s. 17, In this Part ...

"future performance contract" means a contract between a supplier and consumer for the supply of goods or services for which the supply or payment in full of the total price payable is not made at the time the contract is made or partly executed, but does not include

(a) a contract for which the total price payable by the consumer, not including the total cost of credit, is less than a prescribed amount ...

Consumer Contracts Regulation, B.C. Reg. 272/2004, s. 6

The amount of total price payable prescribed for the purposes of the definition of "future performance contract" in section 17 of the Act (definitions — consumer contracts) is $50.

Manitoba—none.

Nova Scotia—NSISCR, s. 2

In addition to the goods and services specified in clause 21W(a) of the Act [goods and services that are immediately downloaded or accessed using the internet], Sections 21X to 21AF of the Act do not apply to goods or services received by a consumer in a transaction where the total costs payable by the consumer to the supplier are less than $50.

Ontario

OCPA, s. 37

Sections 38 to 40 [the internet agreement provisions] apply to an internet agreement if the consumer's total potential payment obligation under the agreement, excluding the cost of borrowing, exceeds a prescribed amount

OCPA Regs., s. 31

The prescribed amount for the purpose of section 37 of the Act is $50.

Additional Exceptions

Alberta

> List of excepted businesses, AFTA, s. 3.

Ontario

> OPCA, s. 2—general exceptions to that Act.

> Part I of the OPCA Regs—"Exemptions from Application of the Act" (ss. 1 to 19), particularly s. 18, which deals with internet agreements.

DISCLOSURE OF INFORMATION

Information Required in Template

3 (1) A supplier must do the following before a consumer enters into an internet sales contract:

(a) disclose to the consumer the following information:

[list of required information]

Provincial Legislation

Alberta—AISCR, s. 4(1) [the list follows as in the *Template*]

British Columbia—BPCPA, s. 46

> (1) A supplier must disclose the following information to a consumer before the consumer enters into a distance sales contract: [requirements refer to information required in other parts of the BPCPA, supplemented by requirements from the Template]

Manitoba—MCPA s. 129

> (1) If a seller fails to provide prescribed information to a buyer in writing before entering into a retail sale or retail hire-purchase agreement with the buyer, the buyer may cancel the agreement

before accepting delivery of the goods or services under the agreement. [Requirements set out IAR, s. 3]

Nova Scotia—NSCPA, s. 21X

Before entering into an internet sales contract with a consumer, a supplier shall disclose the information prescribed by regulations. [Requirements set out NSISCR, s. 3]

Ontario—OCPA, s. 38

(1) Before a consumer enters into an internet agreement, the supplier shall disclose the prescribed information to the consumer. [Requirements set out OCPA, Internet regs s. 32]

Sec. 3(1) ...

(i)   the supplier's name and, if different, the name under which the supplier carries on business;

Provincial Legislation

Alberta—AISCR, s. 4(1)(a)(i)

British Columbia—BPCPA, s. 19(a) [this requirement for future performance and other contracts is also required in distance sales contracts by s. 46(1)(a)]

Manitoba—IAR, s. 3(1)

(a) the seller's name and, if different, the name under which the seller is carrying on business;

Nova Scotia—NSISCR, s. 3(a)

Ontario—OCPA Regs., s. 32

1. The name of the supplier and, if different, the name under which the supplier carries on business.

Sec. 3(1)(a) …

> **(ii)   the supplier's business address and, if different, the supplier's mailing address;**

Provincial Legislation

Alberta—AISCR, s. 4(1)(a)(ii)

British Columbia—BPCPA, s. 19(b) [this requirement for future performance and other contracts is also required in distance sales contracts by s. 46(1)(a)]

Manitoba—IAR, s. 3(1)(b)

Nova Scotia—NSISCR, s. 3(b)

Ontario—OCPA Regs., s. 32 …

> 2.   The telephone number of the supplier, the address of the premises from which the supplier conducts business, and information respecting other ways, if any, in which the supplier can be contacted by the consumer, such as the fax number and e-mail address of the supplier.

Sec. 3(1)(a) …

> **(iii) the supplier's telephone number and, if available, the supplier's e-mail address and facsimile number;**

Provincial Legislation

Alberta—AISCR, s. 4(1)(a)(iii)

British Columbia

BPCPA, s. 46(1)(a), which addresses distance sales contracts, adds the requirement from s. 19(c) [future performance and other contracts]:

BPCPA, s. 19 …

(c) the supplier's telephone number and, if available, facsimile number;

BPCPA, s. 46(1) [disclosure for distance sales contracts]:

(b) if available, the supplier's electronic mail address;

Manitoba—IRA, s. 3(1)

(c) the seller's phone number and, if applicable, the seller's fax number and e-mail address;

Nova Scotia—NSISCR, s. 3(c)

Ontario—OCPA Regs. s. 32-2 (as above)

Sec. 3(1)(a) ...

(iv) **a fair and accurate description of the goods or services being sold to the consumer, including any relevant technical or system specifications;**

Provincial Legislation

Alberta—AISCR, s. 4(1)(a)(iv)

British Columbia—BPCPA, s. 46(1) [disclosure for distance sales contracts]

(c) a detailed description of the goods or services to be supplied under the contract, including any relevant technical or system specifications.

Manitoba—IAR, s. 3(1)(d)

Nova Scotia—NSISCR, s. 3(d)

Ontario—OCPA Regs., s. 32

3. A fair and accurate description of the goods and services proposed to be supplied to the consumer, including the technical requirements, if any, related to the use of the goods or services.

Sec. 3(1)(a) ...

   (v)   an itemized list of the price of the goods or services being sold to the consumer and any associated costs payable by the consumer, including taxes and shipping charges;

Provincial Legislation

Alberta—AISCR, s. 4(1)(a)(v)

British Columbia—BPCPA, s. 46(1)(a), which addresses distance sales contracts, adds the requirement from s. 19(f) and (g) [future performance and other contracts]:

   BPCPA, s. 19 ...

   (f)   an itemized purchase price for the goods or services to be supplied under the contract;

   (g)   other costs payable by the consumer, including taxes and shipping charges;

Manitoba—IAR, s. 3(1) ...

   (f)   an itemized list of the price of the goods or services being sold to the buyer, as well as any shipping charges, taxes, customs duties, or broker fees payable by the buyer to the seller;

Nova Scotia—NSISCR, s. 3(e)

Ontario—OCPA Regs., s. 32 ...

   4.   An itemized list of the prices at which the goods and services are proposed to be supplied to the consumer, including taxes and shipping charges.

Sec. 3(1)(a) ...

   (vi) a description of any additional charges that may apply to the contract, such as customs duties and brokerage

fees, whose amounts cannot reasonably be determined by the supplier;

Provincial Legislation

Alberta—AISCR, s. 4(1)(a)(vi)

British Columbia— BPCPA, s. 46(1)(a), which addresses distance sales contracts, adds the requirement from s. 19(h) [future performance and other contracts]:

> BPCPA, s. 19 ...
>
> (h)   if any customs duties, brokerage fees or other additional charges that may apply to the contract cannot reasonably be determined by the supplier, a description of those charges;

Manitoba

> IAR, s. 3(1)(f) (as above) includes customs duties and broker's fees in "itemized list".
>
> IAR, s. 3(1)
>
> (g)   any delivery, handling or insurance costs payable by the buyer in addition to the purchase price of the goods or services;

Nova Scotia—NSISCR, s. 3(f)

Ontario—OCPA Regs., s. 32

> 5.   A description of each additional charge that applies or may apply, such as customs duties or brokerage fees, and the amount of the charge if the supplier can reasonably determine it.

Sec. 3(1)(a) ...

> **(vii)   the total amount of the contract or, where the goods or services are being purchased over an indefinite period, the amount of the periodic payments under the contract;**

Provincial Legislation

Alberta—AISCR, s. 4(1)(a) …

> (vii) the total consideration payable by the consumer to the supplier under the contract or, where the goods or services are being purchased over time, the amount of the periodic payments under the contract;

British Columbia

BPCPA, s. 46(1)(a), which addresses distance sales contracts, adds the requirement from s. 19(j) [future performance and other contracts]:

> BPCPA, s. 19 …

> (j)   the total price under the contract, including the total cost of credit;

BPCPA, s. 46(1)(a), which addresses distance sales contracts, adds the requirement from s. 23(2)(c) [supplementary requirements for future performance contracts]:

> BPCPA, s. 23(2) …

> (c)   if there are periodic payments under the contract, the amount of each of the periodic payments.

Manitoba—IAR, s. 3(1)

> (h)   the total consideration payable by the buyer to the seller under the agreement, and the currency in which it is payable;

Nova Scotia—NSISCR, s. 3(g)

Ontario—OCPA Regs., s. 32

> 6.   The total amount that the supplier knows would be payable by the consumer under the agreement, including amounts that are required to be disclosed under paragraph 5, or, if the goods and services are proposed to be supplied during an indefinite period, the amount and frequency of periodic payments.

Sec. 3(1)(a) ...

(viii) the currency in which amounts owing under the contract are payable;

Provincial Legislation

Alberta—AISCR, s. 4(1)(a)(viii)

British Columbia—BPCPA, s. 46(1) [disclosure for distance sales contracts] ...

>   (d) the currency in which amounts owing under the contract are payable;

Manitoba—IAR, s. 3(1) ...

>   (h) the total consideration payable by the buyer to the seller under the agreement, and the currency in which it is payable;

Nova Scotia—NSISCR, s. 3(h)

Ontario—OCPA Regs., s. 32 ...

>   13. The currency in which amounts are expressed, if it is not Canadian currency.

Sec. 3(1)(a) ...

(ix) the terms, conditions and method of payment;

Provincial Legislation

Alberta—AISCR, s. 4(1)(a)(ix)

British Columbia— BPCPA, s. 46(1)(a), which addresses distance sales contracts, adds the requirement from s. 19(i) [future performance and other contracts]:

>   BPCPA, s. 19 ...

>   (i) a detailed statement of the terms of payment;

Manitoba—IAR, s. 3(1)(i)

Nova Scotia—NSISCR, s. 3(i)

Ontario—OCPA Regs., s. 32 ...

> 7. The terms and methods of payment.

Sec. 3(1)(a) ...

> **(x)   the date when the goods are to be delivered or the services are to begin;**

Provincial Legislation

Alberta—AISCR, s. 4(1)(a) ...

> (x)   the date when the goods are to be delivered or the services are to begin, or both;

British Columbia— BPCPA, s. 46(1)(a), which addresses distance sales contracts, adds the requirement from s. 23(2)(a) and (b) [supplementary requirements for future performance contracts]:

> BPCPA, s. 23(2) ...

> (a)   the supply date;

> (b)   the date on which the supply of the goods or services will be complete;

Manitoba—IAR, s. 3(1) ...

> (k)   the date when the goods are to be delivered or the services are to be commenced;

Nova Scotia—NSISCR, s. 3(j)

Ontario—OCPA Regs., s. 32 ...

> 8. As applicable, the date or dates on which delivery, commencement of performance, ongoing performance and completion of performance would occur.

Sec. 3(1)(a) ...

    (xi) the supplier's delivery arrangements, including the identity of the shipper, the mode of transportation and the place of delivery;

Provincial Legislation

Alberta—AISCR, s. 4(1)(a)(xi)

British Columbia—BPCPA, s. 46(1)(e) [disclosure for distance sales contracts].

Manitoba—IAR, s. 3(1) ...

    (l)   the seller's delivery arrangements, including the method of delivery;

Nova Scotia—NSISCR, s. 3(k)

Ontario—OCPA Regs., s. 32 ...

    9. For goods and services that would be delivered,

        i.   the place to which they would be delivered, and

        ii. if the supplier holds out a specific manner of delivery and intends to charge the consumer for delivery, the manner in which the goods and services would be delivered, including the name of the carrier, if any, and including the method of transportation that would be used.

Sec. 3(1)(a) ...

    (xii) the supplier's cancellation, return, exchange and refund policies, if any;

Provincial Legislation

Alberta—AISCR, s. 4(1)(a)(xii)

British Columbia—BPCPA, s. 46(1)(f)

Manitoba—IAR, s. 3(1) …

> (n) the seller's exchange, cancellation and refund policies, if
> applicable;

Nova Scotia—NSISCR, s. 3(l)

Ontario—OCPA Regs., s. 32 …

> 11. The rights, if any, that the supplier agrees the consumer will
> have in addition to the rights under the Act and the
> obligations, if any, by which the supplier agrees to be bound
> in addition to the obligations under the Act, in relation to
> cancellations, returns, exchanges and refunds.

Sec. 3(1)(a) …

> **(xiii) any other restrictions, limitations or conditions of
> purchase that may apply;**

Provincial Legislation

Alberta—AISCR, s. 4(1)(a)(xiii)

British Columbia—BPCPA, s. 19(n) [required for future performance and
other contracts, and also required in distance sales contracts by s.
46(1)(a)]: …

> (n) any other restrictions, limitations or other terms or conditions
> that may apply to the supply of the goods or services;

Manitoba—IAR, s. 3(1) …

> (m) any restrictions or conditions that the seller may apply,
> including geographic limitations for the sale or delivery of the
> goods or services;

Nova Scotia—NSISCR, s. 3(m)

Ontario—OCPA Regs., s. 32 …

14. Any other restrictions, limitations and conditions that would be imposed by the supplier.

Additional Provincial Information Requirements

British Columbia—BPCPA, s. 46(1) [disclosure for distance sales contracts] …

(g) any other prescribed information. [none in *Consumer Contracts Regulation*, B.C. Reg. 272/2004]

Manitoba—IAR, s. 3(1) …

(m) [as above, the requirement to outline geographic limitations for sale or delivery]

(e) details of any warranties or guarantees that apply to the agreement;

…

(j) if credit is extended by the seller,

(i) a description of any security taken by the seller, and

(ii) the information required to be disclosed under Part I of the Act (disclosure of cost of borrowing);

(k) the date when the goods are to be delivered or the services are to be commenced;

…

(o) the seller's policies and arrangements for the protection of the buyer's financial and personal information.

Ontario—OCPA Regs., s. 32

10. For services that would be performed, the place where they would be performed, the person for whom they would be performed, the supplier's method of performing them and, if the supplier holds out that a specific person other than the supplier would perform any of the services on the supplier's behalf, the name of that person.

...

> 12. If the agreement is to include a trade-in arrangement, a description of the trade-in arrangement and the amount of the trade-in allowance.

Express Opportunity to Accept/Decline

Sec. 3(1) ...

(b) provide the consumer with an express opportunity to accept or decline the contract and to correct errors immediately before entering into it.

Provincial Legislation

Alberta—AISCR, s. 4(1)(b)

British Columbia—BPCPA, s. 47 ...

> (2) Before a consumer enters into a distance sales contract that is in electronic form, a supplier must

...

> (b) provide the consumer with an express opportunity
>
> > (i)   to correct errors in the contract, and
> >
> > (ii)   to accept or decline the contract.

Manitoba—no requirement.

Nova Scotia—NSCPA, s. 21Y

> A supplier shall provide the consumer with an express opportunity to accept or decline the internet sales contract and to correct errors immediately before entering into it.

Ontario—OCPA, s. 38 ...

> (2) The supplier shall provide the consumer with an express opportunity to accept or decline the agreement and to correct errors immediately before entering into it.

Required Manner of Disclosure

Sec 3 ...

(2) For the purposes of subsection (1) [information required to be disclosed], a supplier is considered to have disclosed to the consumer the information described in subsection (1)(a) [the list of requirements] if the information is

Provincial Legislation

Alberta—AISCR, s. 4(2)

British Columbia—BPCPA, s. 47(1) ...

(2) Before a consumer enters into a distance sales contract that is in electronic form, a supplier must

(a) make the information required under section 46 [required information for distance sales contracts] available in a manner that

Manitoba—see Manitoba provisions below.

Nova Scotia—NSISCR, s. 4

A supplier is considered to have disclosed to a consumer the information required to be disclosed in Section 3 [list of required information] if ...

Ontario—OCPA, s. 38 ...

(3) In addition to the requirements set out in section 5 [general requirement of comprehensibility], disclosure under this section ["Internet Agreements"] shall be accessible and shall be available in a manner that ensures that,

Clear and Comprehensible

Sec. 3(2)

(a) prominently displayed in a clear and comprehensible manner, and

Provincial Legislation

Alberta—AISCR, s. 4(2)(a)

British Columbia—BPCPA, s. 46

> (2) The supplier must disclose the information required under subsection (1) [for distance sales contracts] in a clear and comprehensible manner.

Manitoba—no requirement.

Nova Scotia—NSISCR, s. 4

> (a) the information is prominently displayed in a clear and comprehensible manner;...

Ontario—OCPA, s. 5 ["disclosure of information"—applies to the entire OCPA]

> (1) If a supplier is required to disclose information under this Act, the disclosure must be clear, comprehensible and prominent.

Information Accessed

Sec. 3(2)(b)

> **(i) the consumer has accessed the information, and**

Provincial Legislation

Alberta—AISCR, s. 4(2)(b)(i)

British Columbia—BPCPA, s. 47(2)(a) ...

> (i) requires the consumer to access the information, and

Manitoba—this provision optional, see below.

Nova Scotia—no similar requirement.

Ontario—OCPA, s. 38(3)(a)

Ability to Print

Sec. 3(2)(b)

   (ii) the consumer is able to retain and print the information.

Provincial Legislation

Alberta—AISCR, s. 4(2)(b)(ii)

Manitoba—this provision optional, see below.

British Columbia—BPCPA, s. 47(2)(a) …

   (ii) allows the consumer to retain and print the information, and

Nova Scotia—NSISCR, s. 4(b)

Ontario—OCPA, s. 38(3)(b)

Manitoba—Required Manner of Disclosure

MCPA, s. 129 …

   (2) For the purpose of subsection (1) [agreement may be cancelled if information not provided], a seller shall be considered to have provided the prescribed information to a buyer in writing if

   (a) the information is sent to the e-mail address provided by the buyer to the seller for the provision of information related to the retail sale or retail hire-purchase agreement; **or**

   (b) the information is made accessible to the buyer on the Internet in a manner that ensures that

      (i) the buyer has accessed the information before entering into the agreement, and

      (ii) the information is capable of being retained and printed by the buyer.

COPY OF INTERNET SALES CONTRACT

Seller Must Provide Copy of Agreement

Sec. 4

(1) A supplier must provide a consumer who enters into an internet sales contract with a copy of the contract in writing or electronic form within 15 days after the contract is entered into.

Provincial Legislation

Alberta—AISCR, s. 5(1)

British Columbia—BPCPA, s. 48

(1) A supplier must give a consumer who enters into a distance sales contract a copy of the contract within 15 days after the contract is entered into.

Manitoba—no similar requirement.

Nova Scotia—NSCPA, s. 21Z(1)

Ontario

OCPA, s. 39

(1) A supplier shall deliver to a consumer who enters into an internet agreement a copy of the agreement in writing within the prescribed period after the consumer enters into the agreement.

OCPA, Regs., s. 33

(1) For the purpose of subsection 39(1) of the Act, the supplier shall deliver a copy of the internet agreement in writing to the consumer within 15 days after the consumer enters into the agreement.

Required Information

Sec. 4

(2) The copy of the internet sales contract under subsection (1) [15 day limit] must include

Provincial Legislation

Alberta—AISCR, s. 5(2)

British Columbia—BPCPA, s. 48(2)

Manitoba—no requirement to provide copy.

Nova Scotia—NSCPA, s. 21Z ...

(2)   A copy of the internet sales contract shall include the requirements prescribed by the regulations.

Ontario—OCPA, s. 39 ...

(2)   The copy of the internet agreement shall include such information as may be prescribed.

Sec. 4(2) [internet sales contract must include]

(a) the information described in section 3(1)(a),

(b) the consumer's name, and

(c) the date the contract was entered into.

Provincial Legislation

Alberta—AFTA s. 5(2)(a) to (c).

British Columbia—BPCPA, s. 48(2)(a) to (c)

Manitoba—no requirement to provide copy.

Nova Scotia—NSISCR, s. 5(1)(a) to (c)

Ontario—OCPA Regs., s. 33(2)1 to 3

Time and Manner for Providing Copy

Sec. 4 ...

(3) For the purposes of subsection (1) [providing a copy in 15 days], a supplier is considered to have provided the consumer with a copy of the internet sales contract if the copy is

Provincial Legislation

Alberta—AISCR, s. 5(3)

British Columbia— BPCPA, s. 48 ...

(3) In addition to section 183(2) [how to give or serve documents generally], the supplier may give a copy of the distance sales contract to the consumer

Manitoba—no requirement to provide copy.

Nova Scotia—NSCPA, s. 21Z

(3) For the purposes of subsection (1), a supplier is considered to have provided a consumer with a copy of the internet sales contract if the copy is sent or otherwise provided in accordance with the regulations. [NSISCR, s. 5(2)].

Ontario—OCPA, s. 39 ...

(3) For the purposes of subsection (1), a supplier is considered to have delivered a copy of the internet agreement to the consumer if the copy is delivered in the prescribed manner.

Sec. 4(3)

(a) sent by e-mail to the e-mail address provided by the consumer to the supplier for the provision of information related to the contract,

Provincial Legislation

Alberta—AISCR, s. 5(3)(a)

British Columbia—see below.

Manitoba—no requirement to provide copy.

Nova Scotia—NSISCR, s. 5(2)(a)

Ontario—OCPA Regs., s. 33(3)

> 1. Transmitting it in a manner that ensures that the consumer is able to retain, print and access it for future reference, such as sending it by e-mail to an e-mail address that the consumer has given the supplier for providing information related to the agreement.

Sec. 4 (1) ...

> **(b) sent by facsimile to the facsimile number provided by the consumer to the supplier for the provision of information related to the contract,**

Provincial Legislation

Alberta—AISCR, s. 5(3)(b)

British Columbia—see below.

Manitoba—no requirement to provide copy.

Nova Scotia—NSISCR, s. 5(2)(b)

Ontario—OCPA Regs., s. 33(3) ...

> 2. Transmitting it by fax to the fax number that the consumer has given the supplier for providing information related to the agreement.

Sec. 4(1) ...

> **(c) mailed or delivered to an address provided by the consumer to the supplier for the provision of information related to the contract,**

Provincial Legislation

Alberta—AISCR, s. 5(3)(c)

British Columbia—see below.

Manitoba—no requirement to provide copy.

Nova Scotia—NSISCR, s. 5(2)(c)

Ontario—OCPA Regs., s. 33(3) ...

> 3. Mailing or delivering it to an address that the consumer has given the supplier for providing information related to the agreement.

Sec 4(1) ...

> **(d) actively transmitted to the consumer in a manner that ensures that the consumer is able to retain the copy, or**

Provincial Legislation

Alberta—AISCR, s. 5(3)(d)

British Columbia—see below.

Manitoba—no requirement to provide copy.

Nova Scotia—no similar provision.

Ontario—no similar provision.

Sec. 4(1) ...

(e) **provided to the consumer in any other manner by which the supplier can prove that the consumer has received the copy.**

Provincial Legislation

Alberta—AISCR, s. 5(3)(e)

British Columbia—BPCPA, s. 48(3) ...

(b) by giving the copy by any other manner that enables the supplier to prove that the consumer has received and retained the copy.

Nova Scotia—NSISCR, s. 5(2)(d)

Ontario—OCPA Regs., s. 33(3) ...

4. Providing it to the consumer in any other manner that allows the supplier to prove that the consumer has received it.

Providing Copy in British Columbia

BPCPA, s. 48 ...

(3) In addition to section 183(2) [how to give or serve documents generally], the supplier may give a copy of the distance sales contract to the consumer

(a) by sending the copy by electronic mail to the electronic mail address provided by the consumer to the supplier for the provision of information related to the contract, or

(b) by giving the copy by any other manner that enables the supplier to prove that the consumer has received and retained the copy.

(4) A copy of the distance sales contract given in accordance with subsection (3) (a) is deemed to be received on the 3rd day after it is sent.

BPCPA, s. 183

(1) This section does not apply to the following:

(a) providing a distance sales contract under section 48 [copy of distance sales contract];

...

(2) All documents that are required or permitted under this Act to be given to or served on a person must be given or served in one of the following ways:

(a) by leaving a copy with the person;

(b) if the person is a consumer, an individual who is the subject of a report, as defined in section 106 [definitions respecting credit reporting], or a debtor,

(i) by leaving a copy at that person's residence with an adult who apparently resides with that person,

(ii) by sending a copy by ordinary mail or registered mail to the address at which that person resides or to a forwarding address provided by that person,

(iii) by leaving a copy in a mail box or mail slot for the address at which that person resides, or

(iv) by attaching a copy to a door or other conspicuous place at the address at which that person resides;

(c) if the person is a supplier or a person not referred to in paragraph (b) [individual subject to credit report or debtor],

(i) by leaving a copy with an agent of that person,

(ii) by sending a copy by ordinary mail or registered mail to the address at which that person carries on business,

(iii) by sending a copy by electronic mail to the electronic mail address provided by that person,

(iv) by leaving a copy in a mail box or mail slot for the address at which that person carries on business, or

(v) by attaching a copy to a door or other conspicuous place at the address at which that person carries on business;

(d) by transmitting a copy to a facsimile number provided as an address for service by the person;

(e) by any other method of service prescribed.

BPCPA, s. 184

A document given or served in accordance with section 183(2) is deemed to be received as follows:

(a) if given or served by sending a copy by ordinary or registered mail, on the 5th day after it is mailed;

(b) if given or served by sending a copy by electronic mail, on the 3rd day after it is sent;

(c) if given or served by leaving a copy in a mail box or mail slot, on the 3rd day after it is left;

(d) if given or served by attaching a copy to a door or other conspicuous place, on the 3rd day after it is attached;

(e) if given or served by transmitting a copy by facsimile, on the 3rd day after it is transmitted;

(f) if given or served by any other method of service prescribed under section 183(2)

CANCELLATION OF INTERNET SALES CONTRACT

Sec. 5

(1) A consumer may cancel an internet sales contract in the following circumstances:

Provincial Legislation

Alberta—AISCR, s. 6(1)

British Columbia—BPCPA, s. 49

> (1) A consumer may cancel a distance sales contract by giving notice of cancellation to the supplier

Manitoba—see cancellation in Manitoba, below.

Nova Scotia—NSCPA, s. 21AA

> A consumer may cancel an internet sales contract under the circumstances described in the regulations.

Ontario—Included with time limit, see below OCPA, s. 40(1).

If Required Information Not Provided

> **Sec. 5(1)**
>
> > **(a) at any time from the date the contract is entered into until 7 days after the consumer receives a copy of the contract if**
> >
> > > **(i) the supplier does not disclose to the consumer the information described in section 3(1)(a) [information disclosure requirements], or**

Provincial Legislation

Alberta—AISCR, s. 6(1)(a)(i)

British Columbia—BPCPA, s. 49(1)

> (a) not later than 7 days after the date that the consumer receives a copy of the contract if
>
> > . . .
> >
> > (ii) the contract does not comply with section 48(2) (required contents of contract),

Manitoba—see cancellation in Manitoba, below.

Nova Scotia—NSISCR, s. 6(1)(a)(i)

Ontario—OCPA, s. 40(1)

(1) A consumer may cancel an internet agreement at any time from the date the agreement is entered into until seven days after the consumer receives a copy of the agreement if,

(a) the supplier did not disclose to the consumer the information required under subsection 38(1) [the prescribed information, CPA Regs., s. 32]; or

---

If Express Opportunity to Accept/Decline Not Provided

Sec. 5(1)(a) ... [consumer may cancel contract until 7 days after if]

(ii) **the supplier does not provide to the consumer an express opportunity to accept or decline the contract or to correct errors immediately before entering into it;**

Provincial Legislation

Alberta—AISCR, s. 6(1)(a)(ii)

British Columbia—BPCPA, s. 49(1)

(a) not later than 7 days after the date that the consumer receives a copy of the contract if

(i) the supplier does not comply with section 47 (distance sales contract in electronic form)[must include opportunity to accept/decline], or

Manitoba—no requirement for opportunity to accept or decline.

Nova Scotia—NSISCR, s. 6(1)(a) ...

(ii) the supplier did not provide the consumer with an express opportunity to accept or decline the contract and to correct errors in accordance with Section 21Y of the Act [which sets out this requirement];

Ontario—OCPA, s. 40(1)

(b) the supplier did not provide to the consumer an express opportunity to accept or decline the agreement or to correct errors immediately before entering into it.

If Supplier Does Not Provide Contract

Sec. 5(1) ... [consumer may cancel a contract:]

(b) within 30 days from the date the contract is entered into if the supplier does not provide the consumer with a copy of the contract pursuant to section 4 [required manner of providing information].

Provincial Legislation

Alberta—AISCR, s. 6(1)(b)

British Columbia—BPCPA, s. 49(1)

(b) not later than 30 days after the date that the contract is entered into if the supplier does not provide the consumer with a copy of the contract in accordance with section 48(1) [within 15 days],

Manitoba—see cancellation in Manitoba, below.

Nova Scotia—NSISCR, s. 6(1)(b)

Ontario—OCPA, s. 40 ...

(2) A consumer may cancel an internet agreement within 30 days after the date the agreement is entered into, if the supplier does not comply with a requirement under section 39 [prescribed time, manner, information; OCPA Regs., s. 33].

Failure to Perform Contract

Where Date Specified

Sec. 5 ...

(2) In addition to the cancellation rights under subsection (1), a consumer may cancel an internet sales contract at any time before delivery of the goods or the commencement of the services under the contract if

(a) in the case of goods, the supplier does not deliver the goods within 30 days from the delivery date specified in the contract or an amended delivery date agreed on by the consumer and the supplier, either in writing or in electronic form, or

(b) in the case of services, the supplier does not begin the services within 30 days from the commencement date specified in the contract or an amended commencement date agreed on by the consumer and the supplier, either in writing or in electronic form.

Provincial Legislation

Alberta

AISCR, s. 6(2)(a)—same as (a) as in *Template,* above.

AISCR, s. 6(2)(b)—see below.

AISCR, s. 6(2) [equivalent to (b) in *Template*] ...

(c) in the case of services other than those services described in clause (b) [see additional grounds, below], the supplier does not begin the services within 30 days from the commencement date specified in the contract or an amended commencement date agreed on by the consumer and the supplier, either in writing or in electronic form.

British Columbia—BPCPA, s. 49

(1) A consumer may cancel a distance sales contract by giving notice of cancellation to the supplier

...

(c) at any time before the goods or services are delivered if the goods or services to be delivered under the contract are not delivered to the consumer within 30 days of the supply date, or

Manitoba—see cancellation in Manitoba, below.

Nova Scotia

NSICSR, s. 6(1)(c)(i)—same as (a) in *Template*, above.

NSICSR, s. 6(1)(c)(ii)—see below.

NSICSR, s. 6(1)(c) [equivalent to (b) in *Template*] ...

(iii) in the case of services, other than those specified in subclause (ii) [see additional grounds, below], the supplier does not begin the services within 30 days from the commencement date specified in the contract or another commencement date agreed on by the consumer and the supplier, either in writing or in electronic form;

Ontario—OCPA, s. 26[1]

(1) A consumer may cancel a future performance agreement at any time before delivery under the agreement or the commencement of performance under the agreement if the supplier,

(a) does not make delivery within 30 days after the delivery date specified in the agreement or an amended delivery date agreed to by the consumer in writing; or

(b) does not begin performance of his, her or its obligations within 30 days after the commencement date specified in the agreement or an amended commencement date agreed to by the consumer in writing.

---

[1] The applicable provisions of the OCPA are for "Future Performance Agreements", which can also apply to "internet agreements" (OCPA, s. 4). In addition to s. 26(1) and (2), which mirror the *Template*, under s. 26(3) "If, after the period in subsection (1) or (2) has expired, the consumer agrees to accept delivery or authorize commencement, the consumer may not cancel the agreement under this section."

Failure to Perform—Additional Provincial Grounds

Alberta—AISCR, s. 6(2) ...

> (b) in the case of travel, transportation or accommodation services, the supplier does not begin the services on the commencement date specified in the contract or an amended commencement date agreed on by the consumer and the supplier, either in writing or in electronic form, or

Nova Scotia—NSICSR s. 6(1)(c) ...

> (ii) in the case of transportation, travel or accommodation services, the supplier does not begin the services on the commencement date specified in the contract or another commencement date agreed on by the consumer and the supplier, either in writing or in electronic form, or

---

Where No Date Specified

Sec. 5 ...

> **(3) If the delivery date or commencement date is not specified in the internet sales contract, a consumer may cancel the contract at any time before the delivery of the goods or the commencement of the services under the contract if the supplier does not deliver the goods or begin the services within 30 days from the date the contract is entered into.**

Provincial Legislation

Alberta—AISCR, s. 6(3)

British Columbia—BPCPA, s. 49

> (1) A consumer may cancel a distance sales contract by giving notice of cancellation to the supplier

> ...

> (d) at any time before the goods or services are delivered if the supply date is not specified in the contract and the supplier

does not deliver the goods or services within 30 days from the date the contract is entered into.

Manitoba—see below.

Nova Scotia—NSISCR, s. 6(1)

(d) at any time before the delivery of the goods or the commencement of the services under the contract, if the delivery date or commencement date is not specified in the internet sales contract and if the supplier does not deliver the goods or begin the services within 30 days from the date the contract is entered into.

Ontario—OCPA, s. 26 ...

(2) If the delivery date or commencement date is not specified in the future performance agreement, a consumer may cancel the agreement at any time before delivery or commencement if the supplier does not deliver or commence performance within 30 days after the date the agreement is entered into.

Cancellation in Manitoba

MCPA, s. 129

(1) If a seller fails to provide prescribed information to a buyer in writing before entering into a retail sale or retail hire-purchase agreement with the buyer, the buyer may cancel the agreement before accepting delivery of the goods or services under the agreement.

MCPA, s. 130

(1) Before accepting delivery of goods or services under a retail sale or retail hire-purchase agreement, the buyer may cancel the agreement if the seller does not

(a) in the case of prescribed goods, deliver the goods by the delivery date specified in the agreement or by any other delivery date agreed to in writing, either on paper or by electronic communication;

   (b) in the case of other goods, deliver the goods within 30 days after

      (i)   the delivery date specified in the agreement or any other delivery date agreed to in writing, either on paper or by electronic communication, or

      (ii) if a delivery date cannot be determined under subclause (i), the date of the agreement;

   (c) in the case of travel, transportation or accommodation services or prescribed services, begin to provide the services on the commencement date specified in the agreement or any other commencement date agreed to in writing, either on paper or by electronic communication; and

   (d) in the case of other services, begin to provide the services within 30 days after the commencement date specified in the agreement or any other commencement date agreed to in writing, either on paper or by electronic communication.

Deemed Delivery of Goods/Commencement of Services

Goods

Delivery Refused

Sec. 5 ...

   (4) For the purposes of subsections (2) [goods not delivered in time] and (3) [delivery date not specified],

      (a) a supplier is considered to have delivered the goods under an internet sales contract if

         (i)   delivery was attempted but was refused by the consumer at the time that delivery was attempted, or

Provincial Legislation

Alberta—AISCR, s. 6(4)(a)(i)

British Columbia—BPCPA, s. 53, For the purposes of this Part [4—Consumer Contracts],

> (a) a supplier is considered to have supplied the goods if
>
>> (i) delivery of the goods was attempted but, at the time of the attempt, the consumer refused delivery, or

Manitoba—MCPA, s. 130(2)

> (2) For the purpose of subsection (1) [cancellation for failure to perform], a seller is deemed to have delivered the goods or services under a retail sale or retail hire-purchase agreement
>
> (a) if delivery was attempted but was refused by the buyer, on the day that delivery was attempted; or ...

Nova Scotia—NSISCR, s. 6(2)(a)

Ontario—see deemed delivery/commencement in Ontario, below.

Delivery Not Possible

Sec. 5(4)(a) ...

> (a) a supplier is considered to have delivered the goods under an internet sales contract if
>
>> ...
>
>> **(ii) delivery was attempted but not made because no person was available to accept delivery for the consumer on the day for which reasonable notice was given to the consumer that the goods were available to be delivered;**

Provincial Legislation

Alberta—AISCR, s. 6(4)(a)(ii)

British Columbia—BPCPA, s. 53, For the purposes of this Part [4—Consumer Contracts],

(a) a supplier is considered to have supplied the goods if

...

(ii) the supplier provided reasonable notice of the delivery and delivery was attempted but did not occur because no person was available to accept delivery for the consumer on the day the delivery was attempted, and

Manitoba—MCPA, s. 130(2)

(b) if delivery was attempted but not made because no person was available to accept delivery for the buyer, on the day that the buyer was given notice that the goods or services are available to be delivered or that the goods are available to be picked up by the buyer.

Nova Scotia—NSISCR, s. 6(2)(b)

Ontario—see deemed delivery/commencement in Ontario, below.

Services

Commencement Refused

Sec 5 ...

(4) For the purposes of subsections (2) [services not commenced] and (3) [starting date not specified],

...

(b) a supplier is considered to have begun the services under an internet sales contract if

(i) commencement was attempted but was refused by the consumer at the time that commencement was attempted, or

Provincial Legislation

Alberta—AISCR, s. 6(4)(b)(i)

British Columbia—BPCPA, s. 53, For the purposes of this Part [4—Consumer Contracts],

> (b) a supplier is considered to have begun delivering the services if
>
> > (i) delivery of the services was attempted but, at the time of the attempt, the consumer refused the services, or

Manitoba—s. 130(2)(a) (as above) refers to goods and services.

Nova Scotia—NSISCR, s. 6(3)(a)

Ontario—see deemed delivery/commencement in Ontario, below.

Commencement Not Possible

> **Sec. 5(4)(b) ... [supplier considered to have commenced services if]**
>
> > **(ii) commencement was attempted but did not occur because no person was available to enable the services to begin on the day for which reasonable notice was given to the consumer that the services were available to begin.**

Provincial Legislation

Alberta—AISCR, s. 6(4)(b)(ii)

British Columbia—BPCPA, s. 53, For the purposes of this Part [4—Consumer Contracts],

> (b) a supplier is considered to have begun delivering the services if
>
> > ...
>
> > (ii) the supplier provided reasonable notice of the delivery and delivery was attempted but did not occur because no person was available to enable the services to begin on the day the delivery was attempted.

Manitoba—s. 130(2)(b) (as above) refers to goods and services

Nova Scotia—NSISCR, s. 6(3)(b)

Ontario—see deemed delivery/commencement in Ontario, below.

Deemed Delivery/Commencement—Ontario

Ontario—OCPA, s. 26 …

(4) For the purposes of subsections (1) [not delivered/commenced as specified] and (2) [date not specified], a supplier is considered to have delivered or commenced performance under a future performance agreement if,

(a) delivery was attempted but was refused by the consumer at the time that delivery was attempted or delivery was attempted but not made because no person was available to accept delivery for the consumer on the day for which reasonable notice was given to the consumer that there was to be delivery; or

(b) commencement was attempted but was refused by the consumer at the time that commencement was attempted or commencement was attempted but did not occur because no person was available to enable commencement on the day for which reasonable notice was given to the consumer that commencement was to occur.

Court May Provide Cancellation Relief

Sec. 6

If in the opinion of the [indicate level of court] it would be inequitable for an internet sales contract to be cancelled under section 5, the court may make any order it considers appropriate.

Alberta

AISCR, s. 7

If in the opinion of the Court it would be inequitable for an internet sales contract to be cancelled under section 6, the Court may make any order it considers appropriate.

AISCR, s. 1 In this Regulation ...

(b) "Court" means the Court of Queen's Bench or, subject to the jurisdiction of the Provincial Court, the Provincial Court;

British Columbia—no equivalent provision.

Manitoba

MCPA s. 131

If in the opinion of a court it would be inequitable for an agreement to be cancelled under section 129 [failure to provide information] or 130 [failure to deliver], the court may make any order it considers appropriate.

MCPA, s. 1(1) In this Act ...

"court" means the Court of Queen's Bench.

Nova Scotia—NSCPA, s. 21AD

A supplier may make an application to the Supreme Court claiming that it would be inequitable for an internet sales contract to be cancelled under Section 21AA and the Court may, upon the application, make any order it considers appropriate.

Ontario—no similar provision. The OPCA does provide, s. 93

(1) A consumer agreement is not binding on the consumer unless the agreement is made in accordance with this Act and the regulations.

(2) Despite subsection (1), a court may order that a consumer is bound by all or a portion or portions of a consumer agreement, even if the agreement has not been made in accordance with this Act or the regulations, if the court determines that it would be inequitable in the circumstances for the consumer not to be bound.

Agreement Cancelled by Notice

Sec. 7

(1) An internet sales contract is cancelled under section 5 on the giving of a notice of cancellation in accordance with this section.

Provincial Legislation

Alberta—AISCR, s. 8(1)

British Columbia—there is no explicit statement to this effect. Section 49(1) states that "A consumer may cancel a distance sales contract by giving notice of cancellation to the supplier", and sections 49(2) [effect of cancellation], 50 [supplier must refund], and 51(1) [consumer must return goods] apply if a distance sales contract is cancelled under s. 49 of that provision.

Manitoba—MCPA, s. 132

> (1) An agreement is cancelled under section 129 [failure to provide information] or 130 [failure to deliver] when a written notice of the cancellation is given in accordance with this section.

Nova Scotia—there is no explicit statement to this effect. NSCPA, s. 21AA provides that "A consumer may cancel an internet sales contract under the circumstances described in the regulations." The NSISCR, do not explicitly note that cancellation is effective on notice, but otherwise provide the circumstances and requirements for such notice as set out in the template.

Ontario—OCPA, s. 94

> (1) If a consumer has a right to cancel a consumer agreement under this Act, the consumer may cancel the agreement by giving notice in accordance with section 92.

> (2) The cancellation takes effect when the consumer gives notice.

Form of Notice

Sec. 7 ...

(2) A notice of cancellation may be expressed in any way as long as it indicates the intention of the consumer to cancel the internet sales contract.

Provincial Legislation

Alberta—AISCR, s. 8(2)

British Columbia—see below.

Manitoba—MCPA s. 132(3) ...

(3) A notice of cancellation is adequate if it indicates the intention of the buyer to cancel the agreement.

Nova Scotia—NSISCR, s. 7

(1) A consumer may notify a supplier of cancellation of their internet sales contract in any manner or form that indicates the consumer's intent to cancel the contract.

Ontario—OCPA, s. 92

(1) If this Act requires a consumer to give notice to a supplier to request a remedy, the consumer may do so by giving notice in accordance with this section.

(2) The notice may be expressed in any way, as long as it indicates the intention of the consumer to seek the remedy being requested and complies with any requirements that may be prescribed.

Sec. 7 ...

(3) The notice of cancellation may be given to the supplier by any means, including, but not limited to, personal service, registered mail, telephone, courier, facsimile and e-mail.

Provincial Legislation

Alberta—AISCR, s. 8(3)

British Columbia—see below.

Manitoba—MCPA, s. 132 ...

>   (2) A buyer may provide a notice of cancellation to the seller by personal delivery or by registered mail, fax, e-mail or any other method by which the buyer can obtain confirmation of delivery of the notice.

Nova Scotia—NSISCR, s. 7 ...

>   (2) Notification pursuant to subsection (1) may be given to the supplier by any means including, but not limited to, personal service, registered mail, telephone, courier, facsimile and e-mail, and when given other than by personal service, is deemed to be given when sent.

Ontario—OCPA, s. 92 ...

>   (3) Unless the regulations require otherwise, the notice may be oral or in writing and may be given by any means.

Form of Notice—British Columbia

BPCPA, s. 54

>   (1) A consumer or supplier may give a notice of cancellation under this Part by any method that permits a person to produce evidence that the consumer or supplier cancelled the contract on a specific date, including
>
>   (a) delivering the notice in person, and
>
>   (b) sending the notice by registered mail, electronic mail or facsimile, to
>
>   (i) the consumer or supplier, as applicable, or

(ii) the postal address, electronic mail address or facsimile number shown in the contract for the person named in the contract as a person to whom notice of cancellation may be given.

(2) A notice of cancellation is sufficient if it indicates, in any way, the intention of the consumer or supplier to cancel the contract and, except in the case of cancellation under sections 21 (1) (direct sales contract—cancellation), 25 (1) (continuing services contract—cancellation) or 26 (3) (time share contract—cancellation), if it states the reason for cancellation.

Notice Deemed Given When Sent

Sec. 7 ...

(4) Where the notice of cancellation is given other than by personal service, the notice of cancellation is deemed to be given when sent.

Provincial Legislation

Alberta—AISCR, s. 8(4)

British Columbia—BPCPA, s. 54 ...

(3) For the purpose of this section [how to give notice of cancellation], a notice of cancellation that is given other than by delivery in person is deemed to have been given at the time it is sent.

Manitoba—MCPA, s. 132

(4) A notice of cancellation that is given otherwise than by personal delivery is deemed to be given when sent.

Nova Scotia—NSISCR, s. 7 ...

(2) Notification pursuant to subsection (1) [consumer need show only intent to cancel] may be given to the supplier by any means including, but not limited to, personal service, registered mail, telephone, courier, facsimile and e-mail, and when given other than by personal service, is deemed to be given when sent.

Ontario—OCPA, s. 92 …

(4) If notice in writing is given other than by personal service, the notice shall be deemed to be given when sent.

Effect of Cancellation

Sec. 8

(1) A cancellation of an internet sales contract under section 5 operates to cancel the contract as if the contract had never existed.

(2) A cancellation of an internet sales contract under section 5 also operates to cancel

(a) any related consumer transaction,

(b) any guarantee given in respect of consideration payable under the contract, and

(c) any security given by the consumer or a guarantor in respect of consideration payable under the contract,

as if the contract had never existed.

(3) Where credit is extended or arranged by the supplier, the credit contract is conditional on the internet sales contract whether or not the credit contract is a part of or attached to the internet sales contract, and if the internet sales contract is cancelled, that cancellation has the effect of cancelling the credit contract as if the internet sales contract had never existed.

Provincial Legislation

Alberta—AISCR, s. 9(1); (2)(a), (b), (c); and (3).

British Columbia—BPCPA does not provide that the contract is cancelled "as if it had never existed" but provides, s. 49 …

(2) If a distance sales contract is cancelled under subsection (1) [conditions of cancellation], the following are also cancelled:

(a) any other related consumer transaction;

    (b) any guarantee given in respect of the total price under the contract;

    (c) any security given by the consumer in respect of the total price under the contract;

    (d) if credit is extended or arranged by the supplier in respect of a distance sales contract, the credit agreement, as defined in section 57 (definitions), whether or not the credit agreement is a part of or attached to the distance sales contract.

Manitoba—MCPA, s. 133

  (1) If an agreement is cancelled under section 129 [failure to provide information] or 130 [failure to deliver],

    (a) every obligation of the buyer under the contract is extinguished; and

Nova Scotia—NSCPA, s. 21AB(1); (2)(a), (b), (c); and (3).

Ontario—OCPA, s. 95[2]

The cancellation of a consumer agreement in accordance with this Act operates to cancel, as if they never existed,

    (a) the consumer agreement;

    (b) all related agreements;

    (c) all guarantees given in respect of money payable under the consumer agreement;

    (d) all security given by the consumer or a guarantor in respect of money payable under the consumer agreement; and

    (e) all credit agreements, as defined in Part VII [Credit Agreements], and other payment instruments, including promissory notes,

---

[2] None of the requirements for "Specific Consumer Agreements" (*i.e.*—Future Performance Agreements or Internet Agreements) apply to Credit Agreements, except in the specific situation where credit was extended to obtain the goods or services from the supplier, in which case it is restricted to the agreement concerning those goods and services and does not apply to the related credit agreement—OCPA Regs 11(1) and (2).

      (i) extended arranged or facilitated by the person with whom the consumer reached the consumer agreement, or

      (ii) otherwise related to the consumer agreement.

Responsibilities On Cancellation

Seller Must Refund

Sec. 9

(1) If an internet sales contract is cancelled under section 5, the supplier must, within 15 days from the date of cancellation, refund to the consumer all consideration paid by the consumer under the contract and any related consumer transaction, whether paid to the supplier or another person.

Provincial Legislation

Alberta—AISCR, s. 10(1)

British Columbia—BPCPA, s. 50

If a distance sales contract is cancelled under section 49, the supplier, within 15 days after the notice of cancellation has been given, must refund to the consumer, without deduction, all money received in respect of the contract and in respect of any related consumer transaction, whether received from the consumer or any other person.

Manitoba—MCPA, s. 133

(1) If an agreement is cancelled under section 129 [failure to provide information] or 130 [failure to deliver],

. . .

    (b) the seller must refund to the buyer, within 30 days after the cancellation, all consideration paid by the buyer under the agreement, whether paid to the seller or any other person.

Nova Scotia—NSCPA, s. 21AC

(1) Where an internet sales contract is cancelled under Section 21AA, a supplier shall, within fifteen days from the date of cancellation, refund to a consumer all consideration paid by the

consumer under the contract and any related consumer transaction, whether paid to the supplier or another person.

Ontario

OCPA, s. 96

(1) If a consumer cancels a consumer agreement, the supplier shall, in accordance with the prescribed requirements,

    (a) refund to the consumer any payment made under the agreement or any related agreement; and

    (b) return to the consumer in a condition substantially similar to when they were delivered all goods delivered under a trade-in arrangement or refund to the consumer an amount equal to the trade-in allowance.

OCPA Regs., s. 79

(1) A supplier who is required to comply with subsection 96(1) of the Act shall do so within 15 days after the day the consumer gives notice to the supplier in accordance with section 92 of the Act that the consumer is cancelling the consumer agreement.

(2) A supplier who is required to return goods to a consumer under clause 96(1)(b) of the Act shall return the goods to the consumer's address.

Consumer Must Return Goods

Time for Return

Sec. 9 ...

(2) If goods are delivered to a consumer under an internet sales contract that is cancelled under section 5, the consumer must, within 15 days from the date of cancellation or delivery of the goods, whichever is later, return the goods to the supplier unused and in the same condition in which they were delivered.

Provincial Legislation

Alberta—AISCR, s. 10(2)

British Columbia—BPCPA, s. 51

(1) If a distance sales contract is cancelled under section 49, the consumer must return any goods received under the contract by delivering the goods

    (a) to the person or place named in the contract as the person to whom or as the place where notice of cancellation may be given, and

    (b) within 15 days after the notice of cancellation has been given or after the goods have been delivered to the consumer, whichever is later.

(2) The consumer must return the goods unused and in the same condition as that in which they were delivered.

Manitoba—see MCPA, s. 133(3)(b) under Manitoba—buyer and seller responsibilities, below .

Nova Scotia—NSCPA, s. 21AC ...

(2) Where goods are delivered to a consumer under an internet sales contract that is cancelled under Section 21AA, the consumer shall, within fifteen days from the date of cancellation or delivery of the goods, whichever is later, return the goods to the supplier unused and in the same condition in which they were delivered.

Ontario

    OCPA, s. 96 ...

(2) Upon cancelling a consumer agreement, the consumer, in accordance with the prescribed requirements and in the prescribed manner, shall permit the goods that came into the consumer's possession under the agreement or a related agreement to be repossessed, shall return the goods or shall deal with them in such manner as may be prescribed.

OCPA Regs., s. 81

(1) This section applies with respect to subsection 96(2) of the Act, if the consumer agreement that has been cancelled is one of the following:

   1. An internet agreement to which sections 38 to 40 of the Act apply.

   2. A remote agreement to which sections 45 to 47 of the Act apply.

   3. A future performance agreement to which sections 22 to 26 of the Act apply.

(2) A consumer who has not received a written direction to destroy the goods under subsection (5) shall return the goods to the supplier's address, by any method that provides the consumer with confirmation of delivery, and shall do so within 15 days after the later of,

   (a) the day the consumer gives notice to the supplier in accordance with section 92 [form of consumer notice] of the Act that the consumer is cancelling the consumer agreement; and

   (b) the day the goods come into the consumer's possession.

Method of Return

Sec. 9 ...

(3) The consumer may return the goods under subsection (2) by any method that provides the consumer with confirmation of delivery to the supplier.

Provincial Legislation

Alberta—AISCR, s. 10(3)

British Columbia—BPCPA, s. 51(3)

Manitoba—see MCPA, s. 133(3)(b) under Manitoba—buyer and seller responsibilities, below.

Nova Scotia—NSCPA, s. 21AC ...

> (3) A consumer may return the goods under subsection (2) by any method that provides the consumer with confirmation of delivery to the supplier.

Ontario

> OCPA Regs., s. 81 ...

> (2) A consumer who has not received a written direction to destroy the goods under subsection (5) shall return the goods to the supplier's address, by any method that provides the consumer with confirmation of delivery and shall do so within 15 days after the later of,

>> (a) the day the consumer gives notice to the supplier in accordance with section 92 [form of consumer notice] of the Act that the consumer is cancelling the consumer agreement; and

>> (b) the day the goods come into the consumer's possession.

Seller Must Accept Return

> **Sec. 9 ...**

> **(4) The supplier must accept a return of goods by a consumer under subsection (2).**

Provincial Legislation

Alberta—AISCR, s. 10(4)

British Columbia—BPCPA, s. 51(4)

Manitoba—MCPA, s. 133 ...

> (4) The seller must accept a return of goods that were returned or refused delivery by a buyer under clause (3)(b).

Nova Scotia—NSCPA, s. 21AC ...

(4) The supplier shall accept a return of goods by a consumer under subsection (2).

Ontario—OCPA Regs., s. 81 ...

(4) The supplier shall be deemed to consent to a return of goods under subsection (2) and is responsible for the reasonable cost of returning the goods.

Seller Must Pay Reasonable Shipping

Sec. 9 ...

(5) The supplier is responsible for the reasonable cost of returning goods under subsection (2).

Provincial Legislation

Alberta—AISCR, s. 10(5)

British Columbia—BPCPA, s. 51(5)

Manitoba—MCPA, s. 133 ...

(5) The seller is responsible for the cost of returning goods under clause (3)(b).

Nova Scotia—NSCPA, s. 21AC(5)

Ontario—also included in OCPA Regs., s. 81(4), as above.

Goods Deemed Returned When Sent

Sec. 9 ...

(6) Goods that are returned by the consumer under subsection (2) otherwise than by personal delivery are deemed for the purposes of that subsection to have been returned when sent by the consumer to the supplier.

Provincial Legislation

Alberta—AISCR, s. 10(6)

British Columbia—BPCPA, s. 51 …

> (6) Goods that are returned by the consumer other than by delivery in person are deemed to have been returned at the time the goods are sent.

Manitoba—MCPA, s. 133 …

> (6) Goods that are returned by the buyer under clause (3)(b) otherwise than by personal delivery are deemed for the purpose of that clause to have been returned when sent by the buyer to the seller.

Nova Scotia—NSCPA, s. 21AC(6)

Ontario—OCPA Regs., s. 81 …

> (3) Goods that are returned under subsection (2) other than by personal delivery shall be deemed to have been returned when sent by the consumer to the supplier.

Manitoba—Buyer and Seller Responsibilities

MCPA, s. 133 …

> (2) If services are provided to a buyer under an agreement after the buyer has cancelled the agreement under section 129 [failure to provide information] or 130 [failure to deliver], the buyer may rescind the notice of cancellation by accepting the services. But the buyer shall not be considered to have rescinded the notice if the services are provided without the buyer being given an opportunity to refuse them.

> (3) If goods are delivered to a buyer under an agreement after the buyer has cancelled the agreement under section 129 [failure to provide information] or 130 [failure to deliver], the buyer may

>> (a) rescind the notice of cancellation by accepting the goods; or

>> (b) refuse to accept delivery of the goods or, having accepted delivery, return the goods, within 30 days after accepting

delivery, to the seller unopened and in the same condition in which they were delivered, by any method that provides the buyer with confirmation of delivery to the seller.

Effect of Cancellation—Additional Requirements

British Columbia—BPCPA, s. 56

If a contract is cancelled under this Part [4—Consumer Contracts], the supplier must cancel any future payments or charges that have been authorized by the consumer.

Ontario

OCPA, s. 96 ...

(3) If a consumer cancels a consumer agreement, the consumer shall take reasonable care of the goods that came into the possession of the consumer under the agreement or a related agreement for the prescribed period.

(4) The consumer owes the obligation described in subsection (3) to the person entitled to possession of the goods at the time in question.

(5) Compliance with this section discharges the consumer from all obligations relating to the goods and the consumer is under no other obligation, whether arising by contract or otherwise, to take care of the goods.

OCPA, Regs., s. 81

(5) In the case of goods that are created, recorded, transmitted or stored in digital form or in other intangible form by electronic, magnetic or optical means or by any other means that has capabilities for creation, recording, transmission or storage similar to those means, a consumer who receives from the supplier a written direction to destroy the goods shall destroy the goods forthwith in accordance with such instructions as may be set out in the direction.

Supplier Right of Action

Sec. 9 ...

(7) Any breach of the consumer's obligations under this section is actionable by the supplier as a breach of statutory duty.

Alberta—AISCR, s. 10(7)

British Columbia—none.

Manitoba—none.

Nova Scotia—NSCPA, s. 21AC(7)

Ontario—OCPA, s. 96(6) ...

> (7) If a consumer has cancelled a consumer agreement and has not met the consumer's obligations under this section, the supplier or the person to whom the obligation is owed may commence an action.

Recovery of Refund

Sec. 10 If a consumer has cancelled an internet sales contract under section 5 and the supplier has not refunded all of the consideration within the 15-day period referred to in section 9(1), the consumer may recover the consideration from the supplier as an action in debt.

Provincial Legislation

Alberta—AISCR, s. 11

British Columbia—BPCPA, s. 55

> If a supplier does not provide a refund as required under Division 2 (direct sales, future performance and time share contracts) or section 50 (distance sales contract), the consumer may recover the refund from the supplier as a debt due.

Manitoba—none.

Nova Scotia—NSCPA, s. 21AE

Ontario

>OCPA, s. 98

>(1) If a supplier has charged a fee or an amount in contravention of this Act or received a payment in contravention of this Act, the consumer who paid the charge or made the payment may demand a refund by giving notice in accordance with section 92 within one year after paying the charge or making the payment.

>(2) A supplier who receives a notice demanding a refund under subsection (1) shall provide the refund within the prescribed period of time. 2004, c. 19, s. 7 (39).

>(3) The consumer may commence an action in accordance with section 100 [in Superior Court] to recover,

>>(a) the payment of a fee or an amount that was charged by the supplier in contravention of this Act; or

>>(b) a payment that was received by the supplier in contravention of this Act.

>OCPA Regs., s. 84

>For the purposes of subsections 98(2) [supplier to provide refund] and (4) [non-supplier] of the Act, the refund shall be provided within 15 days after the day the consumer demands it under subsection 98(1) of the Act.

Credit Card

Consumer May Request Reversal

>**Sec. 11**

>>**(1) A consumer who has charged to a credit card account all or any part of the consideration payable under an internet sales contract or related consumer transaction may request the credit card issuer to cancel or reverse the credit card charge and any associated interest or other charges where the consumer has cancelled the contract under section 5 and the supplier has not refunded all of the consideration within the 15-day period referred to in section 9(1).**

Provincial Legislation

Alberta—AISCR, s. 12(1)

British Columbia—BPCPA, s. 52 ...

(2) A consumer who has charged to a credit card all or any part of the total price under a distance sales contract or any related consumer transaction may request the credit card issuer to cancel or reverse the credit card charge and any associated interest or other charges if the consumer has cancelled the contract under section 49 and the supplier has not refunded all money as required under section 50 [15 day requirement].

Manitoba—MCPA, s. 134

(1) A buyer who has charged to a credit card account all or any part of the consideration payable under a retail sale or retail hire-purchase agreement may request the credit card issuer to cancel or reverse the credit card charge, and any associated interest or other charges, if

   (a) the buyer has cancelled the agreement under section 129 [failure to provide information] or 130 [failure to deliver], and the consideration has not been refunded within the 30-day period referred to in clause 133(1)(b); or

   (b) the agreement is unenforceable because of subsection 20(3) of *The Electronic Commerce and Information Act* and the consideration has not been refunded to the buyer within 30 days after the buyer notified the seller of the error referred to in that subsection.

Nova Scotia—NSCPA, s. 21AF(1)

Ontario—OCPA, s. 99

(1) A consumer who has charged to a credit card account all or any part of a payment described in subsection (2) may request the credit card issuer to cancel or reverse the credit card charge and any associated interest or other charges.

(2) Subsection (1) applies to,

    (a) a payment in respect of a consumer agreement that has been cancelled under this Act or in respect of any related agreement;

    (b) a payment that was received in contravention of this Act;

    (c) a payment in respect of a fee or an amount that was charged in contravention of this Act; and

    (d) a payment that was collected in respect of unsolicited goods or services for which payment is not required under section 13 [relief from obligations—unsolicited goods].

(3) A consumer may make a request under subsection (1) if the consumer has cancelled a consumer agreement or demanded a refund in accordance with this Act, and the supplier has not refunded all of the payment within the required period.

Required Form of Request

Sec. 11 ...

(2) A request under subsection (1) must be in writing or electronic form and contain the following information:

Provincial Legislation

Alberta—AISCR, s. 12(2)

British Columbia—the form is not prescribed, but particular information is required under the BPCPA, s. 52 ...

    (3) The request under subsection (2) must contain the following information:

Manitoba—the form is not prescribed, but particular information is required under the IAR, s. 5,

    A buyer's request under section 134 of the Act to cancel or reverse a credit card charge in respect of an Internet agreement must include the following information:

Nova Scotia—NSCPA, s. 21AF ...

(2) A request under subsection (1) shall be in writing or electronic form and shall

  (a) contain the requirements prescribed by the regulations; and

  (b) be made within any time period prescribed by the regulations.

Ontario—OCPA Regs., s. 85 ...

(2) For the purpose of subsection 92(2) of the Act, a request by a consumer to a credit card issuer under subsection 99(1) of the Act shall be signed by the consumer and shall set out the following information:

_____

Required Information

Sec. 11(2) ...

  (a) the consumer's name;

  (b) the consumer's credit card number;

  (c) the expiry date of the consumer's credit card;

  (d) the supplier's name;

  (e) the date the internet sales contract was entered into;

  (f) the dollar amount of consideration charged to the credit card account in respect of the internet sales contract and any related consumer transaction;

  (g) a description of the goods or services sufficient to identify them;

  (h) the reason for cancellation of the internet sales contract under section 5;

  (i) the date and method of cancellation of the internet sales contract.

Provincial Legislation

All of the provinces, except Nova Scotia, require more information than the *Template*:

Alberta—AISCR, s. 12(2) (a) thru (i); the Alberta regulation adds s. 12(2) …

> (j) a statement that the consumer did not receive a refund from the supplier in accordance with section 10(1) [as an action in debt].

British Columbia—BPCPA, s. 52(3) …

> (a) the supplier's name;
>
> (b) the date the distance sales contract was entered into;
>
> (c) the amount charged to the credit card in respect of the distance sales contract and any related consumer transaction;
>
> (d) a description of the goods or services sufficient to identify them;
>
> (e) the reason for cancellation under section 49, of the distance sales contract;
>
> (f) the date and method of cancellation of the distance sales contract.

Manitoba—IAR, s. 5

> (a) the buyer's name and address;
>
> (b) the number and expiry date of the buyer's credit card number;
>
> (c) the seller's name;
>
> (d) information sufficient to identify the credit card charge sought to be cancelled or reversed;
>
> (e) a statement that

(i)   the agreement has been cancelled under section 129 or 130 of the Act and the cancellation has not been rescinded, or

(ii) the agreement is unenforceable because of subsection 20(3) of *The Electronic Commerce and Information Act.*

Nova Scotia—NSISCR, s. 8(a) to (i).

Ontario—OCPA Regs., s. 85(2) ...

1.   The name of the consumer.

2.   The number of the consumer's credit card account.

3.   The expiry date set out on the consumer's credit card.

4.   The name of the supplier who was required to make the refund.

5.   If known, the date of the consumer agreement, if any, between the consumer and the supplier.

6.   Each charge to the consumer's credit card account that the consumer is requesting the credit card issuer to cancel or reverse, including,

     i.   the amount of the charge,

     ii.   the date the charge was posted, and

     iii. a description of the consumer transaction that resulted in the charge.

7.   If the charge to be cancelled or reversed relates to a payment in respect of a consumer agreement that has been cancelled under the Act,

     i.   a statement to that effect,

     ii.   the date the agreement was cancelled, and

     iii. the method used by the consumer to give the supplier notice of cancellation.

8. If the charge to be cancelled or reversed relates to a payment that was received in contravention of the Act,

    i.   a statement to that effect,

    ii. the date the consumer demanded the refund, and

    iii. the method used by the consumer to give the supplier notice demanding the refund.

9. If the charge to be cancelled or reversed relates to a payment that was collected in respect of unsolicited goods or services for which payment is not required under section 13 of the Act,

    i.   a statement to that effect,

    ii. the date the consumer demanded the refund, and

    iii. the method used by the consumer to give the supplier notice demanding the refund.

Obligations of Credit Card Issuer

Acknowledge Request

Sec. 11 ...

(3) The credit card issuer must

(a) acknowledge the consumer's request within 30 days of receiving it, and

Provincial Legislation

Alberta—AISCR, s. 12(3)(a)

British Columbia—BPCPA, s. 52(4)(a)

Manitoba—no requirement for credit card issuer to acknowledge request.

Nova Scotia—NSCPA, s. 21AF(4)(a)

Ontario

    OCPA, s. 99 …

    (5) The credit card issuer,

        (a) shall, within the prescribed period, acknowledge the consumer's request; and

    OCPA Regs., s. 85 …

    (3) For the purpose of clause 99(5)(a) of the Act, the credit card issuer shall acknowledge the consumer's request within 30 days after the day the consumer's request is given to the credit card issuer in accordance with section 92 of the Act.

Reverse Charge

    Sec. 11(3) …

        (b) if the request meets the requirements of subsection (2), cancel or reverse the credit card charge and any associated interest or other charges within 2 complete billing cycles of the credit card issuer or 90 days, whichever first occurs.

Provincial Legislation

Alberta—AISCR, s. 12(3)(b).

British Columbia—BPCPA, s. 52(4)(b)

Manitoba—MCPA, s. 134 …

    (2) On receiving a request under subsection (1) that satisfies prescribed requirements, the credit card issuer must cancel or reverse the credit card charge and any associated interest or other charges.

Nova Scotia—NSCPA, s. 21AF(4) …

        (b) where the request satisfies subsections (2) [required form and information] and (3) [affidavit, if requested, see additional requirements below], cancel or reverse the credit card charge and any associated interest or other charges within two complete billing cycles of the credit card issuer or ninety days, whichever first occurs.

Ontario—Discretionary Reversal

> OCPA, s. 99 ...

> (5) The credit card issuer,

> [shall acknowledge the request within 30 days, and]

> (b) if the request meets the requirements of subsection (4) [required form, time, information], shall, within the prescribed period,

> > (i) cancel or reverse the credit card charge and any associated interest or other charges, or

> > (ii) after having conducted an investigation, send a written notice to the consumer explaining the reasons why the credit card issuer is of the opinion that the consumer is not entitled to cancel the consumer agreement or to demand a refund under this Act.

> OCPA Regs., s. 85 ...

> (4) For the purpose of clause 99(5)(b) of the Act, the prescribed period begins when the consumer's request is given to the credit card issuer in accordance with section 92 of the Act and ends on the date of the second statement of account that the credit card issuer delivers to the consumer after the consumer's request was given to the credit card issuer.

Form of Request

> **Sec. 11 ...**

> **(4) A request under subsection (1) may be given to the credit card issuer by any means, including, but not limited to, personal service, registered mail, courier, facsimile and e-mail.**

Provincial Legislation

Alberta—AISCR, s. 12(4).

British Columbia—no prescribed form of request.

Manitoba—no prescribed form of request.

Nova Scotia—NSCPA, s. 21AF(5).

Ontario

> OCPA, s. 99 ...

> (4) A request under subsection (1) shall be in writing, shall comply with the requirements, if any, that are prescribed under subsection 92(2), and shall be given to the credit card issuer, in the prescribed period, in accordance with section 92.

> OCPA Regs., s. 85

> (1) For the purpose of subsection 99(4) of the Act, a request by a consumer under subsection 99(1) of the Act shall be given to the credit card issuer within 60 days after the end of the period within which the supplier was required under the Act to refund the payment.

Deemed Given When Sent

Sec. 11 ...

(5) Where the request is given other than by personal service, the request is deemed to be given when sent.

Provincial Legislation

Alberta—AISCR, s. 12(5)

British Columbia—no requirements for form of request.

Manitoba—no requirements for form of request.

Nova Scotia—NSCPA, s. 21AF(6).

Ontario—no similar provision.

Additional Provincial Requirements

Nova Scotia—NSCPA, s. 21AF

> (3) The credit card issuer may, upon receiving a request under subsection (1), require that the consumer verify the content of the request by affidavit or declaration.

Ontario—OCPA, s. 99 …

> (6) A consumer may commence an action against a credit card issuer to recover a payment and associated interest and other charges to which the consumer is entitled under this section.

> (7) If a consumer charges all or part of a payment described in subsection (2) to a prescribed payment system, the consumer may request that the charge be cancelled or reversed and this section applies with necessary modifications to the cancellation or reversal of such a charge.

Offence

12 A contravention of section 9(1) [supplier must refund] or 11(3) [credit card must reverse] is an offence for the purposes of [indicate section of relevant Act].

Provincial Legislation

Alberta

> AISCR, s. 13

> A contravention of section 10(1) [refund] or 12(3) [credit card reversal] is an offence for purposes of section 162 of the Act [non-compliance with regulations].

> AFTA, s. 162,

> (1) A person who contravenes a section in the regulations the contravention of which is designated by the regulations to be an offence is guilty of an offence.

...

(3) The Minister may make regulations designating provisions in the regulations the contravention of which is an offence.

British Columbia—BPCPA, s. 189,

(1) Section 5 of the *Offence Act* (general offence) does not apply to this Act or the regulations.

(2) A person who contravenes subsection (5) or any of the following sections commits an offence:

...

(k) section 46 (1) (disclosure of information respecting distance sales contract);

(l) section 56 (cancellation of preauthorized payments);

Manitoba—MCPA, s. 94

(1) Except where otherwise specifically provided, any person who contravenes, or fails or neglects to comply with, a provision of this Act or the regulations is guilty of an offence and liable, on summary conviction...

Nova Scotia—NSCPA, s. 29

(1) Every person who violates or fails to comply with any provision of this Act or the regulations or an order or direction given under this Act or the regulations and every director of a corporation who knowingly concurs in a violation or failure to comply with any provision of this Act or the regulations or an order or direction given under this Act or the regulations is guilty of an offence and liable on summary conviction to a penalty of not more than two thousand dollars or to imprisonment for a term of not more than one year, or both.

Ontario—OCPA, s. 116

(1) A person is guilty of an offence if the person,

(a) fails to comply with any order, direction or other requirement under this Act; or

...

(2) A person who contravenes or fails to comply with a provision of a regulation made under this Act is guilty of an offence.

(3) An officer or director of a corporation is guilty of an offence if he or she fails to take reasonable care to prevent the corporation from committing an offence mentioned in subsection (1) or (2).

(4) Any person who attempts to commit any offence referred to in subsection (1) or (2) is guilty of an offence.

Additional Provincial Requirements

No Waiver of Rights

Alberta—AFTA, s. 2

(1) Any waiver or release by a person of the person's rights, benefits or protections under this Act or the regulations is void.

(2) Subsection (1) does not apply to a release made by a person in the settlement of a dispute.

British Columbia—BPCPA, s. 3

Any waiver or release by a person of the person's rights, benefits or protections under this Act is void except to the extent that the waiver or release is expressly permitted by this Act.

Manitoba—MCPA, s. 134 ...

(3) This section [credit card reversal] applies despite any agreement to the contrary entered into before or after this Part [XVI, "Internet Agreements"] comes into force.

Nova Scotia—NSCPA, s. 21

This Act applies notwithstanding any agreement or waiver to the contrary.

Ontario

OCPA, s. 7

(1) The substantive and procedural rights given under this Act apply despite any agreement or waiver to the contrary.

OCPA, s. 8

(1) A consumer may commence a proceeding on behalf of members of a class under the *Class Proceedings Act, 1992* or may become a member of a class in such a proceeding in respect of a dispute arising out of a consumer agreement despite any term or acknowledgment in the consumer agreement or a related agreement that purports to prevent or has the effect of preventing the consumer from commencing or becoming a member of a class proceeding.

Review/Expiry

Alberta—AISCR, s. 14

For the purpose of ensuring that this Regulation is reviewed for ongoing relevancy and necessity, with the option that it may be repassed in its present or an amended form following a review, this Regulation expires on September 30, 2016.

3

SECURITY OF PERSONAL INFORMATION

Identity theft has become a major consumer protection issue, and activities over the Internet constitute a major reason for consumer concern. A report prepared by the Public Interest Advocacy Centre ("PIAC") in 2003 highlights that it is mostly a modern crime—a form of fraud that "relies on the commercial culture of ubiquitous personal information holdings, easy consumer credit and the facility of modern technology".[1] Ipsos-Reid has reported that 80 per cent of Canadian adults consider identity theft to be a serious problem.[2]

According to the Consumer Measures Committee in Canada, identity theft is "the use of someone else's personal information, without his or her knowledge or consent, to commit a crime, such as fraud, theft or forgery. Identity theft also includes the acquisition or transfer of personal information as an instrument to commit these crimes in the future".[3] In the consumer context, the growth of the Internet means individuals can shop online, do their banking, and interact with government, all of which usually require the disclosure of personal information such as home address, age, gender, personal identification numbers, credit card numbers, income, employment, assets, liabilities, source of funds, payment records, health records, and e-mail addresses. The Internet provides a new and comprehensive medium for criminals to access this personal data.

The problem is real. According to one study, three per cent of Canadians (approximately 900,000 people) were victims of identity theft in 2003.[4] It is difficult to determine how much of this represents identity theft using the Internet. However, a 2003 Ipsos-Reid Study states that approximately one third of Canadians reported a breach of privacy or

---

[1] Philippa Lawson and John Lawford, "Identity Theft: The Need for Better Consumer Protection" (2003) The Public Interest Advocacy Centre (PIAC) at 5 (hereinafter *PIAC Report*).

[2] Ipsos-Reid, "Concern About Identity Theft Growing in Canada", February 28, 2005, <http://www.ipsos-na.com/news/pressrelease.cfm?id=2582>.

[3] Canada, Consumer Measures Committee, *Working Together to Prevent Identity Theft: A Discussion Paper for Public Consultation* (Ottawa: Industry Canada, June 15, 2005) at 6 (hereinafter *CMC Report*).

[4] Environics Survey quoted in *CMC Report, ibid.*, at 7.

security with respect to the personal information they submitted online. This was a significant increase from the 18 per cent reported in December 2002.[5]

I.   LEGISLATIVE AND COMMON LAW PROTECTION OF PERSONAL INFORMATION

Although there is no generalized offence of "identity theft" in Canada,[6] there are numerous provisions in various statutes that can apply to the wrongful gathering and subsequent misuse of personal information. Statutory solutions, however, may never adequately address the problem. A frequent reason given as a contributing factor to the rise of identity theft is a lack of funding and resources in law enforcement. Consumer awareness and education are also important, as is the maintenance of adequate security standards by organizations that gather large amounts of personal information. The following discussion will consider how existing laws, including common law liability for breach of security of personal information, may be used to combat identity theft.

A.   Criminal Laws Applicable to Identity Theft

The *Criminal Code* contains several provisions that will apply to the misuse of personal information.

---

[5]   See Canada, Consumer *Trends Report*, Electronic Commerce Division of Industry Canada (Ottawa: Electronic Commerce Division of Industry Canada, Office of Consumer Affairs, July, 2005), online: <http://strategis.ic.gc.ca/epic/internet/inoca-bc.nsf/en/ca02096e.html>.

[6]   In the U.S., the *Identity Theft and Assumption Deterrence Act* was enacted in 1998 to address the problem of identity theft and to make it an offence when anyone knowingly transfers or uses, without lawful authority, a means of identification of another person with the intent to commit, or to aid or abet, any unlawful activity that constitutes a violation of federal law, or that constitutes a felony under any applicable State or local law: 18 U.S.C. § 1028(a)(7). Online: <http://www.consumer.gov/idtheft/pdf/penalty_enhance_act.pdf>.

   Critics of the Act say that identity theft has grown considerably since its enactment because enforcing its provisions has proved to be difficult. Some argue that the Act is ineffective because it targets the wrong side of the problem by attempting to deter identity thieves with strong penalties. This is said to be ineffective because the chance of being caught is so slight. Some suggest that the fight against identity theft should instead target the source of the problem — the prevalence of unsecured personal information — by tightening up laws on the protection of such information. See R.B. McMahon, "After Billions Spent to Comply with HIPAA and GLBA Privacy Provisions, Why is Identity Theft the Most Prevalent Crime in America?" (2004) 49 Villanova L.R. 624. Most states have also enacted criminal identity theft statutes.

• Subsection 342(3) criminalizes the possession, use of or trafficking in credit card and debit card data in such a way that would allow the perpetrator to use either the credit card or debit card itself or to obtain the services provided by the issuer of the card.[7]

• Section 380 deals with fraudulent conduct and applies where a person defrauds another of property, money, or valuable security or any service. Penalties can include imprisonment for up to ten years for frauds of over $5,000 and up to two years in jail for frauds under that amount.[8]

• Identity thieves may in some cases also be guilty of the offence of impersonation under s. 403 of the *Criminal Code*.[9] Section 362 deals with obtaining credit by a false pretence or by fraud, and knowingly making a false statement with intent that it be relied upon, for the purpose of procuring the delivery of property or the payment of money, the making of a loan, or the granting or extending of credit.

• The forgery provisions (ss. 366–378) apply to persons who make false documents with intent to use them for a variety of related activities. Use of forged documents to defraud another person qualifies as fraud and uttering a forged document. The making, executing, drawing, signing,

---

[7] R.S.C. 1985, c. C-46, s. 342(3):

Every person who, fraudulently and without colour of right, possesses, uses, traffics in or permits another person to use credit card data, whether or not authentic, that would enable a person to use a credit card or to obtain the services that are provided by the issuer of a credit card to credit card holders is guilty of

(a) an indictable offence and is liable to imprisonment for a term not exceeding ten years; or (b) an offence punishable on summary conviction.

[8] *Ibid.*, at s. 380(1):

Every one who, by deceit, falsehood or other fraudulent means, whether or not it is a false pretence within the meaning of this Act, defrauds the public or any person, whether ascertained or not, of any property, money or valuable security or any service,

(a) is guilty of an indictable offence and liable to a term of imprisonment not exceeding fourteen years, where the subject-matter of the offence is a testamentary instrument or the value of the subject-matter of the offence exceeds five thousand dollars; or

(b) is guilty

(i) of an indictable offence and is liable to imprisonment for a term not exceeding two years, or

(ii) of an offence punishable on summary conviction, where the value of the subject-matter of the offence does not exceed five thousand dollars.

[9] *Ibid.*, s. 403:

Every one who fraudulently personates any person, living or dead,

(a) with intent to gain advantage for himself or another person,

(b) with intent to obtain any property or an interest in any property, or

(c) with intent to cause disadvantage to the person whom he personates or another person,

is guilty of an indictable offence and liable to imprisonment for a term not exceeding ten years or an offence punishable on summary conviction.

accepting or endorsing of a document in the name or on the account of another person, if done with the intent to defraud the person, is an offence under s. 374.

• With respect to online identity theft, the harvesting of personal information by means of unauthorized access to a computer system may be captured by s. 342.1(1)[10] (see the discussion on "phishing", *infra.*).

Despite the availability of these provisions, the tackling of identity theft, particularly online identity theft, is not adequately served by criminal legislation that was not designed for this specific purpose. For example, it would not be an offence under the *Criminal Code* to possess multiple pieces of identification for several people (absent proof of theft or forgery), or to merely possess an individual's personal information with intent to commit a crime. The manufacturing and possession of "novelty" identification is also not an offence. The *PIAC Report* states that law enforcement officials cite the lack of an offence for simple possession of false or multiple identification as a significant challenge to the application of the *Criminal Code* provisions to combat identity theft.[11]

Other legislation that outlaws activities associated with identity theft includes the *Employment Insurance Act*, which makes it an offence to knowingly apply for more than one social insurance number ("SIN"), use another person's SIN to deceive or defraud, loan or sell a SIN or a SIN card to deceive or defraud, or to manufacture a phoney SIN card. The Act provides penalties of a fine up to $1,000 and/or imprisonment for up to one year.[12] As well, a number of provincial statutes contain offences that may apply to identity theft-related activities. For example, under the Nova Scotia *Vital Statistics Act*,[13] it is an offence to obtain or attempt to obtain a

---

[10] *Ibid.*, s. 342.1(1):

Every one who, fraudulently and without colour of right,

(*a*) obtains, directly or indirectly, any computer service,

(*b*) by means of an electro-magnetic, acoustic, mechanical or other device, intercepts or causes to be intercepted, directly or indirectly, any function of a computer system,

(*c*) uses or causes to be used, directly or indirectly, a computer system with intent to commit an offence under paragraph (*a*) or (*b*) or an offence under section 430 in relation to data or a computer system, or

(*d*) uses, possesses, traffics in or permits another person to have access to a computer password that would enable a person to commit an offence under paragraph (*a*), (*b*) or (*c*)

is guilty of an indictable offence and liable to imprisonment for a term not exceeding ten years, or is guilty of an offence punishable on summary conviction.

[11] Philippa Lawson and John Lawford, "Identity Theft: The Need for Better Consumer Protection" (2003) The Public Interest Advocacy Centre (*PIAC Report*), at 35.

[12] S.C. 1996, c. 23, s. 141(1) and (2).

[13] R.S.N.S. 1989, c. 494.

birth certificate or a copy of the registration of a birth for a fraudulent or other improper purpose.

B.   Privacy Legislation

One could argue that Canada's relatively recent privacy protection legislation, and its provincial counterparts, could be used to combat identity theft. However, privacy legislation was not designed for this purpose, and constitutes an awkward tool in this regard. The federal *Personal Information Protection and Electronic Documents Act* (*"PIPEDA"*)[14] governs the collection, use and disclosure of personal information by organizations in Canada in the course of commercial activity. Alberta, Quebec and British Columbia are exempt from *PIPEDA*, because they have passed provincial legislation that is substantially similar to it.

Among the protections in *PIPEDA* and its provincial counterparts that are relevant to the prevention of identity theft include:

*   a prohibition against organizations from collecting an individual's personal information without consent unless authorized by the Act;
*   a requirement that collection and disclosure of personal information be limited to specified purposes;
*   a requirement that organizations meet standards of accuracy; and
*   a requirement that organizations keep information within their control secure.

Ironically, some of the requirements designed to protect personal information in *PIPEDA* could work against businesses' efforts to verify identity. For example, Principle 4.4 states that the collection of personal information must be limited to that which is necessary for the purposes identified by the organization. In one finding[15] of the Privacy Commissioner of Canada, a telecommunications company that required several pieces of identification from prospective customers argued that such measures were necessary in order to prevent identity fraud. But the Commissioner found that only two pieces of identification were necessary to establish identity and that the company was in violation of Principle 4.4.

PIPEDA has been criticized for having a weak, cumbersome mechanism for ensuring privacy protection. The application of its

---

[14]   S.C. 2000, c. 5.
[15]   *PIPEDA* Case Summary #288, online: <http://www.privcom.gc.ca/cf-dc/2005/288_050201_e.asp>.

principles to protect against identity theft similarly provides very little assurance to consumers.

C.   Consumer Reporting Legislation

Like consumer protection, consumer reporting services are generally regulated by provincial legislation. Most provinces in Canada offer a series of similar protections against unauthorized access to credit information.[16]

For example, the Nova Scotia *Consumer Reporting Act*[17] establishes a consumer's rights related to consumer or credit reports. It imposes accuracy standards on credit reporting bureaus and limits the disclosure of credit information to authorized recipients. It also provides rights to victims or potential victims of identity theft such as allowing consumers to examine the content of their consumer file, including the names of people who requested consumer reports in the previous 12 months, and copies of any written reports made to any person.[18] Ontario's *Consumer Reporting Act*[19] limits the rights of parties to obtain individual names from a credit bureau and places obligations on a credit bureau to notify consumers prior to providing such information to third parties.[20] It also requires credit reporting agencies to investigate consumer complaints of inaccuracies, correct inaccuracies and report such corrections to anyone who was provided with the consumer's credit report during the previous two months.[21]

Provincial consumer reporting legislation has been criticized as being largely ineffective in protecting victims and potential victims of identity theft, particularly in the Internet era. For example, the *PIAC Report* provides the following comments:

> … consumers are typically not informed at the time that unfavourable credit information is placed on their file. It is unclear what efforts, if any, credit bureaus make to corroborate such information, even where required by law. And there is no requirement for credit bureaus to obtain proof of customer consent before releasing personal information to third parties. Nor are credit bureaus required to notify consumers of possible fraudulent activity when, for example, numerous credit applications are

---

[16] New Brunswick does not have consumer reporting legislation.
[17] R.S.N.S. 1989, c. 93; as amended by S.N.S. 1999, c. 4, ss. 10-16.
[18] *Ibid.*, s. 12.
[19] R.S.O. 1990, c. C.33.
[20] *Ibid.*, s. 11.
[21] *Ibid.*, s. 13.

submitted within a short time period. The onus is instead on consumers to review their credit reports periodically in order to check for fraudulent activity.[22]

D. Legislative Reform

Although existing Canadian legislation contains a diverse set of measures that can be used to target identity theft, they do not adequately address the uniqueness of the problem. Technological advancements now permit vast storehouses of electronic data, which can lead to consequences of enormous scope if the security of the data is compromised. Consequently, there is growing pressure for Canada to enact legislation requiring businesses to notify consumers when they have reason to believe that the security of consumer personal information has been compromised.[23] Such legislation has been passed in the United States,[24] which has resulted in significant spending by organizations to improve the security of personal information within their control.[25] The U.S. requirements are also having a spillover effect into Canada.[26]

The only legislative data protection requirement in Canada is the obligation under Principle 7 of *PIPEDA* and its provincial counterparts that adequate safeguards be in place appropriate to the sensitivity, amount, distribution, format of the information collected, and the method of storage.[27] The consequences, however, of breaching this Principle are minimal. For example, the Privacy Commissioner's office does not have the power to levy fines or penalties, and often does not name the offending organization in its reported findings.

---

[22] Philippa Lawson and John Lawford, "Identity Theft: The Need for Better Consumer Protection" (2003) The Public Interest Advocacy Centre *(PIAC Report)* at 36.

[23] For example, see M. Geist, "Pressure Builds for Privacy Breach Disclosure Law" *Toronto Star* (July 4, 2005).

[24] See, for example, the State of California's *Database Breach Notification Act*, Cal. Civ. Code paras. 1798.29, 1798.82 and 1789.84, which require organizations to provide notice to any California resident whose private electronic data is suspected to have been compromised. This legislation, effective on July 1, 2003, was the first of its kind in North America.

[25] See B. Wright, "Internet break-ins: new legal liability" (2004) 20:3 Computer L. and Security Report at 164.

[26] For example, Equifax Canada sent notice to 1400 Canadians, even though it was unclear that any of the data subjects were protected by California's law. See J. Evers, "Canadian credit agency reports data breach", *CNET News.com* (June 16, 2005), online: <http://news.com.com/2102-1029_3-5750434.html?tag=st.util.print>.

[27] Schedule 1 to the *Personal Information Protection and Electronic Documents Act*, S.C. 2000, c. 5.

A legislated reporting requirement, similar to existing U.S. measures, is in the early stages of discussion in Canada. In 2005, the Consumer Measures Committee, a multi-jurisdictional group organized in 2004, released a discussion paper on identity theft for public consultation.[28] The *CMC Report* suggests several reforms that would make it harder for identity thieves to access personal information, make it easier to monitor and detect identity theft, and make it easier for victims of identity theft to minimize damage.[29] The *CMC Report* does not address prosecution issues, nor does it consider Internet-related identity theft specifically. The suggested reforms include:[30]

- a requirement that persons who accept payment cards (including credit cards and debit cards) for the transaction of business not print the expiry date or more than the last five digits of the card number on any receipt generated electronically at the point of sale or transaction;
- a requirement that credit bureaus take reasonable steps to authenticate the people and organizations that access credit reports;
- a prohibition on financial institutions and consumer reporting agencies from using a SIN as a unique identifier for consumers or from disclosing a SIN on a credit report;
- a requirement allowing consumers to place freezes on their credit reports so that they may not be released to third parties without the authorization of the consumer;
- a requirement that organizations that store personal information notify individuals and credit bureaus in cases of security breaches;
- a requirement that credit bureaus place fraud alerts on consumers' credit reports in cases of security breaches or upon the request of an identity theft victim;
- a requirement that credit lenders disclose details of fraudulent debts to victims;
- a requirement that credit bureaus block information about fraudulent debts from appearing on a consumer's credit report;
- making organizations liable for damages for failing to comply with the above.

---

[28] Consumer Measures Committee, *Working Together to Prevent Identity Theft: A Discussion Paper for Public Consultation* (Ottawa: Industry Canada, 2005) (hereinafter *CMC Report*).
[29] *Ibid.*, at 11.
[30] *Ibid.*, at 12-25.

E.   Common Law Liability

The *CMC Report* suggests that a statutory cause of action should be considered, which would not require proof of specific damages.[31] Such a statutory right would likely be necessary for consumers seeking a civil action, as tort law appears to be inadequate for this purpose. Attempts in the United States to establish the tort of "negligent enablement" have usually failed, and it is similarly unlikely to succeed in the United Kingdom.[32] In a recent case from South Carolina, that state's Supreme Court held that several financial institutions that issued credit cards in the plaintiff's name to an imposter owed no duty of care to the plaintiff.[33] The court stated: "the relationship, if any, between credit card issuers and potential victims of identity theft is far too attenuated to rise to the level of a duty between them. Even though it is foreseeable that injury may arise by the negligent issuance of a credit card, foreseeability alone does not give rise to a duty."[34]

With respect to allegations of inadequate security of personal information, consumers may have a stronger claim, although as of this writing there is no such established common law action.[35] As discussed earlier, organizations do have a responsibility under *PIPEDA* to secure personal information, which perhaps could be used as support in establishing a duty of care. One could also argue that a Web site that promises to provide high security standards (by, for example, applying a security "seal" for consumer confidence) must meet the high standard promised as a condition of any contract entered into with the business operating the Web site.

---

[31]   *Ibid.*, at 23. Although consumers who are victims of identity theft relating to credit cards seldom suffer significant actual losses because of limitations in credit card agreements and legislation, they do suffer significant inconvenience and usually some out-of-pocket expenses in attempting to undo the damage of identity theft.

[32]   Toby Blyth, "Banker's Liability for Negligent Enablement of Imposter Fraud and Identity Theft" (2004) 19:2 *Journal of International Banking Law and Regulation* 40 [Westlaw: J.I.B.L.R. 2004, 19(2), 40-44].

[33]   *Huggins v. Citibank, N.A.*, S.E.2d 275, 2003 WL 21910366, (Sup. Ct., S.C. 2003).

[34]   *Ibid.*, at 334.

[35]   In *Lac Minerals Ltd. v. International Corona Resources*, [1989] S.C.J. No. 83, [1989] 2 S.C.R. 574, the Supreme Court of Canada held that where a party receives private information in confidence, there is an expectation that it will not misuse that information for its own benefit and where the information has a commercial value and is given in the course of a business relationship, the recipient is bound by an obligation of confidence. However, the action may require an element of *active* "unauthorized use" by the vendor as opposed to merely allowing the information to be held in an insecure setting.

Consumers who make allegations of negligence for breach of security standards would be confronted with the most recent judgment from the Supreme Court of Canada on the elements of duty of care,[36] which at least one commentator suggests could be an impediment on the ability of negligence law to adapt to technology-based relationships.[37] According to the Supreme Court, one must scrutinize the relationship between plaintiff and defendant for factors indicating "closeness" that make it "just and fair" to impose a duty of care, and further consider policy factors that might negate a duty of care even if foreseeability and "closeness" are established.[38] In a situation, for example, where a vendor sends personal information that it collects to a third party for processing or storage, and that third party's security is compromised, it is difficult to ascertain whether there is or should be any expectation or reliance upon which one can make a finding of "closeness". And given that courts are also concerned about indeterminate liability in tort, policy reasons may also override other considerations.

Because Canadian law does not currently provide a legislative duty to notify when the security of personal information is compromised, consumers would be forced to argue that there is a duty to notify them under principles of common or civil law. As of this writing, a class action lawsuit has been launched against the Canadian Imperial Bank of Commerce, alleging that the bank failed to maintain adequate security and privacy of its customers' personal information, and failed to warn its customers of a security breach when customer information was faxed repeatedly to third parties without consent. Coupled with the issues addressed in the *CMC Report,* the stage may be set in Canada for future developments in consumer protection against identity theft.[39]

F.   Legal Implications of Privacy and Security "Seals"

A particular perspective on Internet regulation that is especially prevalent in the business sector calls for minimal government intrusion, most notably with respect to electronic commerce. Promoters of self-regulation abhor legislative intervention in privacy, security or online

---

[36]   *Cooper v. Hobart,* [2001] S.C.J. No. 76, 206 D.L.R. (4th) 193.

[37]   Robert J. Currie, "Of Neighbours and Netizens, or, Duty of Care in the Tech Age: A Comment on *Cooper v. Hobart* (2004) 3 Canadian Journal of Law and Technology 81 at 84.

[38]   *Ibid.,* at 83.

[39]   A copy of the Statement of Claim is available online: <http://www.cacounsel.com/ CIBC%20Class%20Action%20Claim.pdf>.

consumer protections, and argue that a self-regulatory model that rewards businesses that abide by good business practices and standards is the most efficient and expedient way to promote electronic commerce and provide customer satisfaction.

In furtherance of the self-regulatory model, it has become popular for Web sites to carry various "seals" of approval. Consumers who encounter such seals on a Web page are supposed to have their fears of lack of privacy or security assuaged, as the Web site business has been "certified" as meeting best practice standards.[40]

The public accounting profession was one of the first organizations to provide independent verification that an online business is meeting good business standards. The "WebTrust" seal provided through the Canadian Institute of Chartered Accountants is meant to provide a visual assurance in the electronic commerce arena "that an entity's systems meet rigorous security, privacy, processing integrity, availability, or confidentiality standards. The seals convey to end-users, customers and others that the associated entity has met or exceeded high standards regarding the protection of their customers' private information, integrity of transactions, availability of the system, etc."[41]

Another organization that provides Web seals, TRUSTe, markets itself as "an independent, nonprofit organization dedicated to enabling individuals and organizations to establish trusting relationships based on respect for personal identity and information in the evolving networked

---

[40]   The most common Web seals include TRUSTe (<http://www.truste.org>), WebTrust (<http://www.webtrust.net>), Better Business Bureau's BBBOnline (<http://www.bbbonline.com>) and VeriSign (<http://www.verisign.com>). The type and degree of assurances provided by each seal vary.

   The concept has also been adopted in other online contexts. For example, the Open Source Initiative has adopted a graphic certification mark that "certifies" that software is being distributed under a licence that conforms to the Initiative's Open Source definition. See the Open Source Initiative Web site: <http://www.opensource.org/docs/certification_mark.php>.

[41]   The Canadian Institute of Chartered Accountants, "International Seal Usage", 2004, online: <http://www.aicpa.org/download/trust_services/AICPA-CICA_Usage_Guide.pdf>.

   According to AICPA/CICA, successful qualification for the WebTrust seal indicates that an organization's standards meet certain criteria, and that ongoing adherence to these standards is necessary to keep the seal:

   If your systems and processes meet the requirements of a Trust Services assurance engagement that results in an unqualified report by your practitioner, your organization will be eligible to begin using the appropriate Trust Services Seal(s). The Trust Services seals represent compliance with the highest standards and practices, and adherence to these standards is required to continue using the seals. (at 41)

world".[42] The TRUSTe "trustmark" certifies that online companies comply with their own stated privacy policies.

Unfortunately for consumers, the Web seal assurances have not prevented serious breaches of security and the release of personal information by many businesses that have carried Web seals of approval. Indeed, the seal providers have been criticized for failing to monitor Web site businesses that are granted a seal, relying too heavily on consumers and privacy advocates to report privacy violations, and being apologists for businesses that violate the privacy standards promised by the seals.[43]

The impact, or lack thereof, of Web seals on privacy and security standards was highlighted in 2000 in the American case *FTC v. Toysmart.com, LLC.*[44] The online toy retailer Toysmart went bankrupt, and listed its most valuable asset as its customer information database. While in business, Toysmart.com had collected detailed personal information about its customers, including names, addresses, billing information, shopping preferences, and family profiles. The company had a privacy policy that assured its customers that their personal information would never be shared with third parties, and its Web site carried the TRUSTe seal of assurance.

TRUSTe did ultimately inform the Federal Trade Commission ("FTC") of Toysmart.com's apparent violation of its own privacy policy, but the case underlined a fundamental problem with online privacy seals: the lack of effective recourse by the organization itself against violators who carry the seal.[45] TRUSTe, for example, appears to depend primarily on third parties for enforcement, such as the FTC in the Toysmart case. At best, Web certifiers have served as "watchdogs", but rarely ensure that there is ongoing compliance unless breaches are explicitly brought to their attention. At worst, organizations that provide Web seals have been criticized for creating a dangerous illusion of privacy protection, and for being apologists for businesses that violate privacy and security policies.[46]

The justification for this latter criticism is evident in the facts of a 2006 settlement reached between New York State and the e-mail

---

[42] Online: <http://www.truste.org>.

[43] See, for example, "Free IPod Takes Privacy Toll", Wired News, March 16, 2006, online: <http://wired.com/news/technology/1,70420-0.html>.

[44] 2000 U.S. Dist. LEXIS 21963 (D. Mass. 2000).

[45] D. Bronski, C. Chen, M. Rosenthal and R. Pluscec, *FTC v. Toysmart*, 2001 Duke Law & Tech. Rev. 0010.

[46] See, for example, "Free IPod Takes Privacy Toll", Wired News, March 16, 2006, online: <http://wired.com/news/technology/1,70420-0.html>.

marketing company Datran Media.[47] Datran purchased personal customer information from companies with explicit privacy policies that indicated such information would not be sold or transferred to third parties. The largest purchase, involving 7.2 million names, was from Gratis Internet, whose network of sites prominently displayed the TRUSTe seal. TRUSTe initially defended Gratis Internet, and stated that the company did not violate its privacy policy. Subsequently TRUSTe revoked Gratis' seal, later reinstated it, and revoked it again, without publicly declaring its reasons for doing so.[48]

The lack of obvious accountability of Web certifiers leads one to question whether the assurances provided by their seals could be actionable in tort by consumers who rely on these assurances. The "expectation gap" faced by the accounting profession, which refers to the difference between the auditor's role perceived by investors and creditors and the role held by the auditors themselves, may be relevant in the Web seal context, particularly since the accounting profession has been a leader in the Web seal arena with the WebTrust seal.[49] Fundamentally, a court would have to ascertain whether a Web seal may reasonably be interpreted as providing to online consumers a high level of assurance that their personal information will be protected in accordance with an organization's privacy and security policies. The understanding of the Web seal provider may reflect something significantly less than the provision of such an assurance.

Although no reported legal cases have addressed the issue of the liability of Web seal providers to consumers, there has been some suggestion that mere foreseeability of reliance and harm will not suffice under the law of most jurisdictions of the United States.[50] It has also been suggested that recent decisions from the Supreme Court of Canada that raise public policy arguments against the imposition of indeterminate liability for pure economic loss in Canada would apply in the Web seal context.[51]

---

[47] See the press release of the Office of the New York Attorney General, "Investigation Reveals Massive Privacy Breach", March 13, 2006, online: <http://www.oag.state.ny.us/press/2006/mar/mar13a_06.html>.

[48] See, for example, "Free IPod Takes Privacy Toll", Wired News, March 16, 2006, online: <http://wired.com/news/technology/1,70420-0.html>.

[49] See C. Pacini and D. Sinason, "Auditor Liability for Electronic Commerce Assurance: the CPA/CA Webtrust (1999) 36 American Business Law Journal 479.

[50] Ibid.

[51] Carl Pacini, David Sinason, Dominic Peltier-Rivest, "Assurance Services and the Electronic Frontier: The International Legal Environment of the CPA/CA WebTrust" (1999) 12 Advances in International Accounting.

In 1997 the Supreme Court of Canada issued its decision in *Hercules Managements Ltd. v. Ernst & Young*,[52] which remains the leading decision in Canada on the tortious liability of auditors to third parties. The Supreme Court unanimously decided that investors should generally not be able to recover against a corporation's auditors whose financial reports are prepared for a corporation in which they invested. The court adopted a two-part test in its examination of whether auditors owed investors a duty of care. First, an examination of "proximity" must be undertaken, in which it is determined whether the auditor had an obligation to be mindful of the plaintiff investors' legitimate interests. According to La Forest J.,

> To my mind, proximity can be seen to inhere between a defendant-representor and a plaintiff-representee when two criteria relating to reliance may be said to exist on the facts: (a) the defendant ought reasonably to foresee that the plaintiff will rely on his or her representation; and (b) reliance by the plaintiff would, in the particular circumstances of the case, be reasonable.[53]

The court in the circumstances concluded that the auditors satisfied the first part of the test, and that a *prima facie* duty existed.

The second part of the test examines policy considerations that may limit or even deny recovery. The court emphasized the economic repercussions of exposing auditors to indeterminate liability, and concluded that liability should be denied, principally for this policy reason. The court also highlighted the practical consequences of imposing broad liability in these circumstances, such as increased professional liability insurance premiums that could lead to structural changes in the insurance industry, and took note that a finding of liability would encourage investors to be "free riders" who would lack incentive to exercise vigilance.[54]

What does the Supreme Court's position on the liability of auditors have to do with Web seal providers? It has been suggested by some writers that the same considerations will apply to accountants who provide the WebTrust seal to insulate them from liability.[55] The "proximity"

---

[52]   [1997] S.C.J. No. 51, [1997] 2 S.C.R. 165.

[53]   *Ibid.*, at para. 24.

[54]   For a critique of the *Hercules Managements* decision, see M. Deturbide, "Liability of Auditors: *Hercules Managements Ltd. et al. v. Ernst & Young et al.*" (1998) 77 Can. Bar Rev. 260.

[55]   See Carl Pacini, David Sinason, Dominic Peltier-Rivest, "Assurance Services and the Electronic Frontier: The International Legal Environment of the CPA/CA WebTrust" (1999) 12 Advances in International Accounting.

analysis in *Hercules Managements* may indicate that Web seal providers should reasonably foresee consumer reliance on their seals, and such reliance may be reasonable (although the "expectation gap" discussed above would be relevant in this analysis). Indeed, it may be that in most cases a duty to consumers can be established.[56] However, the policy considerations that vitiated the duty of care of auditors would arguably also apply to Web seal providers: a concern over liability in an indeterminate amount to an indeterminate class, a resultant structural impact on electronic commerce, and the reliance of consumers on "free ridership" in place of a diligent examination of the privacy and security policies of organizations with which they do business.

However, a direct analogy of Web seal providers, even if they are accountants, to auditors is problematic. Auditors are engaged by corporations to provide reports for a variety of reasons, including the fact that audited financial statements may be required under corporate or securities legislation, and the board of directors, in fulfilling its duties to the corporation, requires some assurance of managerial responsibility. Although privacy legislation such as the *Personal Information Protection and Electronic Documents Act* requires organizations, including online businesses, to protect personal information, they are not legally required to have a privacy audit or a seal of approval affixed to their Web site assuring compliance with any privacy standards. Rather, the fundamental reason for doing so is to provide assurances to third parties that the Web site adheres to appropriate privacy and security standards. For example, the WebTrust marketing information indicates that the presence of the WebTrust seal "reduces concerns of consumers, businesses, and business customers so you acquire and retain business" and "can convert shoppers into online buyers".[57] When a consumer clicks the TRUSTe seal on a Web site that displays it, he or she is directed to a statement on TRUSTe's Web site that indicates the privacy practices of that business have been reviewed by TRUSTe "for compliance with its strict program requirements".[58]

As to the "free ridership" concern, both the courts and legislatures in Canada have long recognized that consumers are entitled to more protections in law than other purchasers in the marketplace. The "buyer beware" principle has been diminished by both consumer protection legislation and by judicial interpretation of doctrines such as

---

[56] *Ibid.*
[57] Online: <http://www.webtrust.org/why_have_engagement.htm>.
[58] See, for example, the privacy policy of Air Canada, see online: <http://www.aircanada.com>.

unconscionability with respect to limitation of liability.[59] In short, consumers should be able to "free ride" on representations, like those made by Web seal providers, that induce them to transact business over Web sites that carry those representations.

Finally, the policy considerations that may limit or even deny recovery, as articulated by the court in *Hercules Managements,* cannot be applied convincingly to the Web seal context. The business of providing Web seals is not so entrenched that the imposition of liability for misrepresentation would open the floodgates of litigation, lead to structural changes in the marketplace, and have a negative impact on the economy.

Given the volume of high-profile privacy and security breaches, and the criticism levied against Web seal providers for their ineffectiveness in monitoring organizations that carry their seals, it may be argued that it is the Web seal providers who are receiving a "free ride" of non-accountability. Although a satisfactory statutory action for breach of privacy and security is still lacking,[60] the potential common law liability for misrepresentation of third parties such as Web seal providers may provide an alternative remedy, but remains to be tested by the courts.

There has been some suggestion that governments should get into the Web seal business as a means of attracting electronic commerce to their jurisdictions by providing certain assurances to consumers. For example, a report prepared for the Ontario Ministry of Consumer and Commercial Relations in 2000 suggested the adoption of a trust mark "which would be instantly recognizable by consumers and provide them with a heightened level of assurance that the site in question meets provincial licensing and regulatory requirements".[61] The report acknowledges that an "aggressive" monitoring program for non-compliance would be necessary to protect consumers who would rely on the seal.[62] The proposed initiative has not been implemented, perhaps due to resource implications or possible liability concerns.

A 2000 Joint Project of the Office of the Information and Privacy Commissioner of Ontario and the Office of the Federal Privacy Commissioner of Australia examined the effectiveness of the three

---

[59] Although, as we have seen, the Ontario courts have been less willing to examine these issues in the online context. See Chapter 1.

[60] See the discussion on legislative reform in Part D, above.

[61] M. Geist, "Consumer Protection and Licensing Regimes Review: The Implications of Electronic Commerce" (2000) Report to the Ontario Ministry of Consumer and Commercial Relations, online: <http://aix1.uottawa.ca/~geist/mccrgeist.pdf>, at 11.

[62] *Ibid.,* at 13.

leading online privacy seals: BBBOnLine, TRUSTe and WebTrust.[63] The Joint Project evaluated several criteria to determine whether Web seals were effective tools that online users could use to protect their personal data, and reached the unhelpful conclusion that "the precise role that seals can fill in providing acceptable and enforceable privacy protection for a consumer's transaction on a Web site is still unclear".[64] The Report found that a strong privacy law in any jurisdiction was a consumer's primary protection, and that a Web seal would be most relevant in providing additional protection that exceeded statutory standards.

The Privacy Commissioners found that none of the seals that they evaluated required their participants to meet all of the Guidelines developed by the Organisation for Economic Co-operation and Development ("OECD") on the protection of privacy and transborder flows of personal data,[65] the international standard against which the privacy principles of the various Web seals were being compared. For example, the seal providers did not require the businesses carrying their seals to restrict their use of personal information to that which was relevant and necessary for the purposes for which the data was collected. Nevertheless, it was concluded that "seals are playing a valuable educational role in promoting privacy awareness in the minds of both consumers and businesses alike".[66] The potential accountability of the seal providers to consumers was not directly addressed.

II. "PHISHING"

The previous discussion focused on the negligence of other parties that release personal information that could then be used for a fraudulent purpose. But sometimes it is consumers who may unwittingly provide their personal information to deceitful individuals. This is especially true online, where a nefarious activity labelled "phishing" has entered the lexicon.

"Phishing" is a general term for the "creation and use of e-mails and websites — designed to look like e-mails and websites of well known

---

[63] "Web Seals: A Review of Online Privacy Programs" (2000) The Office of the Information and Privacy Commissioner/Ontario and The Office of the Federal Privacy Commissioner of Australia, online: <http://www.privacy.gov.au/publications/seals.html>.

[64] *Ibid.*, s. 5.2.

[65] Available online: <http://www.oecd.org>.

[66] "Web Seals: A Review of Online Privacy Programs" (2000) The Office of the Information and Privacy Commissioner/Ontario and The Office of the Federal Privacy Commissioner of Australia, online: <http://www.privacy.gov.au/publications/seals.html>, Executive Summary.

legitimate businesses, financial institutions, and government agencies — in order to deceive Internet users into disclosing their bank and financial account information or other personal data such as usernames and passwords".[67] A variant of phishing is "pharming", which involves hacking into a Web site and redirecting that Web site's traffic to another Web site.[68]

The term "phishing" refers to the fact that Internet fraud artists use e-mail lures to "fish" for passwords and financial data from the sea of Internet users. The term has been in use since 1996 when hackers were accessing America On-Line accounts by stealing passwords from unsuspecting AOL users.[69] The classifications and variants of phishing schemes are constantly changing, and range from casting a wide net to catch naive consumers who trustingly provide personal information such as bank account numbers, to sophisticated attacks that take the victim to a fraudulent Web site while displaying the address of the true Web site in the browser's window.[70]

Much phishing activity is related to unsolicited e-mail, or "spam", which, in Canada, is not directly regulated through legislation. However, a federal task force on spam made several recommendations in its 2005 Report which could also be used to target phishing.[71] These recommendations are highlighted in the following discussion on legislative solutions to the problem of phishing.

---

[67] Canada, *Public Advisory — Phishing: An Emerging Trend in Identity Theft* (Public Safety and Emergency Preparedness Canada, 2004), online: <http://ww2.psepc-sppcc.gc.ca/publications/policing/phishing_e.asp>, at 1; United States, *Special Report on "Phishing"* (Department of Justice, 2004), online: <http://www.usdoj.gov/criminal/fraud/Phishing.pdf>, at 3.

[68] See online: <http://en.wikipedia.org/wiki/Pharming>.

[69] See the Anti-Phishing Working Group Web page on the origins of the term "phishing", online: <http://www.antiphishing.org/word_phish.html>.

[70] See A. Emigh, "Online Identity Theft: Phishing Technology, Chokepoints, and Countermeasures" (2005), online: <http://www.antiphishing.org/>.

[71] Canada, Task Force on Spam, *Report of the Task Force on Spam, Stopping Spam: Creating a Stronger, Safer Internet* (Ottawa: Task Force on Spam, Industry Canada, May, 2005), online: <http://e-com.ic.gc.ca/epic/internet/inecic-ceac.nsf/vwapj/stopping_spam_May2005.pdf/$file/stopping_spam_May2005.pdf> (hereinafter *Task Force on Spam Report*).

A.   Existing Legislation Applicable to Phishing

1.   *PIPEDA*[72]

PIPEDA and its provincial counterparts would apply to organizations that send out unsolicited commercial bulk e-mail,[73] the instrument of many phishing schemes. The Act defines "personal information" as "information about an identifiable individual, but does not include the name, title or business address or telephone number of an employee of an organization".[74] E-mail addresses are not specified in s. 2 and are therefore personal information for the purpose of the Act. Further, Principle 4.3 of Schedule 1 – Consent, states that:

> The knowledge and consent of the individual are required for the collection, use, or disclosure of personal information, except where inappropriate.

However, an organization may collect and use personal information without the knowledge or consent of the individual if the information is publicly available and is specified in the regulations.[75] The regulations specify that publicly available information includes the name, title, address and telephone number of an individual that appears in a professional or business directory, listing or notice, that is available to the public, where the collection, use and disclosure of the personal information relate directly to the purpose for which the information appears in the directory, listing or notice.[76] In a recent decision involving spam, the Privacy Commissioner of Canada ruled that a business e-mail address is personal information protected under *PIPEDA*.[77] "Address harvesting" by spammers for phishing purposes would therefore be captured by *PIPEDA*, which prohibits the collection, use or disclosure of personal information (e-mail addresses) without consent.[78]

---

[72] S.C. 2000, c. 5.

[73] Canada, Task Force on Spam, *Report of the Task Force on Spam, Stopping Spam: Creating a Stronger, Safer Internet* (Ottawa: Task Force on Spam, Industry Canada, May, 2005), online: <http://e-com.ic.gc.ca/epic/internet/inecic-ceac.nsf/vwapj/stopping_spam_May2005.pdf/$file/stopping_spam_May2005.pdf> (hereinafter *Task Force on Spam Report*).

[74] S.C. 2000, c. 5, s. 2.

[75] *Ibid.*, s. 7(1)(*d*).

[76] *Regulations Specifying Publicly Available Information*, SOR/2001-7, December 13, 2000.

[77] *PIPEDA* Case Summary #297, Issued December 1, 2004, online: <http://www.privcom.gc.ca/cf-dc/2005/297_050331_01_e.asp>.

[78] Task Force on Spam, *Report of the Working Group on Legislation and Enforcement*, online: <http://e-com.ic.gc.ca/epic/internet/inecic-ceac.nsf/en/h_gv00337e.html>.

However, *PIPEDA*'s utility in combating phishing is limited. Phishing activities are notorious for being difficult to trace. As discussed earlier, *PIPEDA* has been criticized for lacking strength for its designed purpose, protection of privacy. It is an even weaker instrument with which to tackle phishing. Even in situations where phishers are identifiable, *PIPEDA* would involve expensive and lengthy applications to the Federal Court to seek a penalty or obtain an award of damages since the Commissioner's office does not have order-making powers.

The Task Force on Spam Background Report made the following comments on the limitations of *PIPEDA* in combating spam. The comments would apply equally to phishing:

> While PIPEDA addresses the issue of consent for the collection, use and disclosure of personal information such as e-mail addresses, the Working Group has found that there are limitations in the ways in which the legislation can respond to the problem of spam. Given the transitory nature of spam, and the continuous evolution in the ways in which these spammers work, it is important that a new law allow for timely reaction and responsive, agile, quick enforcement.[79]

2.   *Competition Act*[80]

To the extent that the *Competition Act* regulates false or misleading representations,[81] its application to spam that misleads consumers could also catch phishing activities. However, the provisions under the *Competition Act* that deal with the misleading content of messages may not address header information, and the pursuit of such an offence would currently be unlikely to lead to successful prosecution.[82]

3.   *Criminal Code*

Phishing is a form of fraud, and therefore subject to the fraud provisions in the *Criminal Code*. In addition to the provisions of the *Criminal Code* discussed earlier with respect to identity theft, additional offences may be applicable to phishing schemes. Section 372(1) applies to individuals who send false messages with the intent to injure:

---

[79] *Ibid.*

[80] R.S.C. 1985, c. C-34.

[81] *Ibid.*, s. 52(1).

[82] *Regulations Specifying Publicly Available Information*, SOR/2001-7, December 13, 2000.

§372(1) Every one who, with intent to injure or alarm any person, conveys or causes or procures to be conveyed by letter, telegram, telephone, cable, radio or otherwise information that he knows is false is guilty of an indictable offence and liable to imprisonment for a term not exceeding two years.[83]

Section 342.1, dealing with unauthorized access to a computer system, could be applied to spammers and phishers who access computer servers without permission for the purpose of harvesting e-mail addresses:

§342.1(1) Every one who, fraudulently and without colour of right,

(*a*) obtains, directly or indirectly, any computer service,

(*b*) by means of an electro-magnetic, acoustic, mechanical or other device, intercepts or causes to be intercepted, directly or indirectly, any function of a computer system,

(*c*) uses or causes to be used, directly or indirectly, a computer system with intent to commit an offence under paragraph (*a*) or (*b*) or an offence under section 430 in relation to data or a computer system, or

(*d*) uses, possesses, traffics in or permits another person to have access to a computer password that would enable a person to commit an offence under paragraph (*a*), (*b*) or (*c*)

is guilty of an indictable offence and liable to imprisonment for a term not exceeding ten years, or is guilty of an offence punishable on summary conviction.

"Computer service" includes data processing and the storage or retrieval of data.[84]

Although potentially applicable, the provisions in the existing federal statutes identified above would be limited in their effectiveness in combating phishing due to the difficulty in identifying the perpetrators and in enforcing the legislation. The *Task Force on Spam Report* makes the following finding with respect to enforcement of legislation against spam. The comment is equally applicable to enforcing existing legislation against phishing:

The enforcement agencies face a number of challenges related to the use of their legislation to address all the various elements of the spam problem. Limited resources and competing priorities are significant factors hindering the two regulatory bodies involved, as well as the RCMP and local law enforcement agencies. A further impediment to effective enforcement is the frequent lack of specialized technical

---

[83] R.S.C. 1985, c. C-46, s. 372(1).
[84] *Ibid.*, s. 342.1(2).

expertise needed to track down, investigate and prosecute spammers. Finally, in many cases, existing enforcement powers have not yet been used, and the legislative tools to attack particular elements of spam are either too uncertain in their application or simply missing.[85]

The Task Force further determined that existing legislation had significant gaps for combating more aggressive and invasive spam and spam-related activities like phishing. The deterrence aspects of existing legislation were also found wanting with respect to malicious conduct such as phishing.[86]

B. Legislative Reform

The Canadian government has been slow to address the problem of spam, and the related issue of phishing, with the result that Canada lags behind most industrialized countries that have targeted spam and phishing legislatively.[87] However, several of the recommendations contained within the *Task Force on Spam Report* are relevant to phishing, in particular Recommendations 2 and 3:[88]

2. The federal government should establish in law a clear set of rules to prohibit spam and other emerging threats to the safety and security of the Internet (e.g. botnets, spyware, keylogging) by enacting new legislation and amending existing legislation as required.

3. To this end, the following e-mail activities and practices should be made offences in spam-specific legislation (these provisions may also be reflected, in whole or in part, in existing legislation):

---

[85] Canada, Task Force on Spam, *Report of the Task Force on Spam, Stopping Spam: Creating a Stronger, Safer Internet* (Ottawa: Task Force on Spam, Industry Canada, May, 2005), online: <http://e-com.ic.gc.ca/epic/internet/inecic-ceac.nsf/vwapj/stopping_spam_May2005.pdf/$file/stopping_spam_May2005.pdf> (hereinafter *Task Force on Spam Report*), at 12.

[86] *Ibid.*, at 13.

[87] See, for example, the European Union Directive 2002/58/EC on Privacy and Electronic Communications; and the U.S. federal *CAN-SPAM Act*, 19 U.S.C.§ 1037.

With respect to targeting identity theft and phishing specifically, several pieces of legislation have been tabled in the United States: *Anti-phishing Act of 2005*, S. 472, 109th Cong. (2005); H.R. 1099, 109th Cong. (2005); *Notification of Risk to Personal Data Act of 2005*, S. 751, 109th Cong. (2005); *Comprehensive Identity Theft Prevention Act of 2005*, S. 768, 109th Cong. (2005); *Consumer Data Security and Notification Act of 2005*, H.R. 3140, 109th Cong. (2005); *Financial Privacy Breach Notification Act of 2005*, S. 1216, 109th Cong. (2005); *Notification of Risk to Personal Data Act 2005*, S. 1326, 109th Cong. (2005).

[88] Canada, Task Force on Spam, *Report of the Task Force on Spam, Stopping Spam: Creating a Stronger, Safer Internet* (Ottawa: Task Force on Spam, Industry Canada, May, 2005), online: <http://e-com.ic.gc.ca/epic/internet/inecic-ceac.nsf/vwapj/stopping_spam_May2005.pdf/$file/stopping_spam_May2005.pdf>.

- the failure to abide by an opt-in regime for sending unsolicited commercial e-mail;
- the construction of false or misleading headers or subject lines (i.e. false transmission information) designed to disguise the origins, purpose or contents of an e-mail, whether the objective is to mislead recipients or to evade technological filters;
- constructing false or misleading URLs and websites for the purpose of collecting personal information under false pretences or engaging in criminal conduct (or to commit other offences listed);
- the harvesting of e-mail addresses without consent, as well as the supply, use or acquisition of such lists; and
- dictionary attacks.

The Task Force recommends that the new offences should be strict liability offences with criminal liability for more egregious or repeated offences. The Task Force also recommends a private right of action, available to both individuals and corporations, with meaningful statutory damages available.[89] The response of government to these recommendations remains to be seen.

A recent legislative effort directed at telemarketing could also provide the impetus for a similar effort to combat spam and its consequent effects. The *Telecommunications Act*[90] has been amended to provide the Canadian Radio-television and Telecommunications Commission ("CRTC") with the authority to establish a national do-not-call list ("DNCL") and to delegate the administration of the DNCL and related functions to a third party. The amended Act also gives the CRTC the right to impose administrative monetary penalties for violations of its telemarketing rules. The amendments received royal assent on 25 November 2005, and came into force on June 30, 2006.[91]

However, a do-not-spam equivalent to a DNCL presents practical concerns, as identified by the U.S. Federal Trade Commission's ("FTC") 2004 Report to Congress.[92] The FTC determined that spammers would most likely use a registry as a mechanism for verifying the validity of e-mail addresses, and that efforts were better spent ending the anonymity of spammers by ensuring that a message actually comes from the domain name indicated in the e-mail header. The FTC also highlighted the dangers associated with identifying do-not-spam accounts for children, which could be used by pedophiles to target children.

---

[89] *Ibid.*, at 14.

[90] S.C. 1993, c. 38.

[91] S.C. 2005, c. 50; SI/2006-0070.

[92] National Do Not E-mail Registry: A Report to Congress, Federal Trade Commission, 2004, online: <http://www.ftc.gov/reports/dneregistry/report.pdf>.

III. IDENTITY THEFT EDUCATION AND PREVENTION EFFORTS

Since consideration of a legislative response is at an early stage, it is clear that consumers themselves must be cognizant of the risks associated with divulging their personal information in suspicious circumstances. Most reports which have concluded that a legislative response is required for online consumer protection issues have also highlighted a need for consumers to take affirmative measures to protect themselves.[93] Among the various public- and private-sponsored education and prevention efforts focusing on identity theft include:

- The Consumer Measures Committee ("CMC"), a multi-jurisdictional working group created in 2004 to examine consumer issues such as identity theft. The CMC provides publications such as identity theft checklists for consumers and businesses, and tips for reducing the risk of identity theft.[94]

- The Competition Bureau of Canada's international anti-fraud public education campaign, adopted for use in the United States and United Kingdom.[95]

- A joint Public Advisory on Identity Theft, issued by Public Safety and Emergency Preparedness Canada (formerly the Department of the Solicitor General of Canada) and the U.S. Department of Justice.[96]

- The Canadian Bankers Association ("CBA") best practices regarding the use of online resources for conducting personal financial transactions.[97]

- PhoneBusters, a national anti-fraud call centre jointly operated by the Ontario Provincial Police and the RCMP. PhoneBusters is the central agency in Canada that collects information on telemarketing, advanced fee fraud letters and identity theft complaints. It also provides a variety of consumer information on identity theft.[98]

---

[93] For example, Canada, Task Force on Spam, *Report of the Task Force on Spam, Stopping Spam: Creating a Stronger, Safer Internet* (Ottawa: Task Force on Spam, Industry Canada, May, 2005), online: <http://e-com.ic.gc.ca/epic/internet/inecic-ceac.nsf/vwapj/stopping_spam_May2005.pdf/$file/stopping_spam_May2005.pdf> at 24.

[94] See CMC identity theft working group website, online: <http://cmcweb.ca/epic/internet/incmc-cmc.nsf/en/fe00084e.html>.

[95] See press release online: "Competition Bureau to Spearhead First International Anti-Fraud Public Education Campaign – Canada, U.S. and U.K. Urge Consumers to Recognize, Report and Stop Fraud" at <http://www.ic.gc.ca>.

[96] Available online: <http://www.psepc.gc.ca>.

[97] Available online: <http://www.psepc.gc.ca>.

[98] Available online: <http://www.phonebusters.com/english/recognizeit_identitythe.html>.

4

SPYWARE AND MALWARE

I. INTRODUCTION

The emergence into the lexicon of the terms "malware" and "spyware" reflects one of the many sinister aspects of the Internet. Both consumers and businesses have been victims of online technological pestilence, which is often created maliciously or for fraudulent purposes, and may be subsequently propagated intentionally or unintentionally. Such invasive software can trigger a host of problems, resulting in consequences ranging from mere annoyances to catastrophic system failures. Most computers connected to the Internet have experienced some symptoms of infection, which may frequently be manifested simply by a slowing down of a computer's processing ability.

The nomenclature used to classify invasive software varies according to its function and *modus operandi*.[1] Collectively, malicious software is referred to as "malware". Viruses, worms, and Trojan horses are all forms of malware that can cause serious damage to a computer. Viruses and worms attach to a program or file, or embed within a computer, and spread to other computers via the Internet. Trojan horses masquerade as legitimate software that, when downloaded and opened, can create havoc by, for example, deleting or re-ordering files.

More recently, another type of invasive software, labelled "spyware", has become endemic. Spyware gathers information about a person or organization without their knowledge. On the Internet, spyware is surreptitiously installed on computers to secretly gather information about the computer user and relay it to advertisers or other interested parties. Although some may consider spyware to be principally a form of data mining, and therefore rather innocuous compared with traditional malware, it should be noted that some forms of spyware may be used for fraudulent purposes, and *all* forms compromise a computer user's privacy. Despite the fact that some forms of spyware can have as devastating effects to a consumer as any form of malware, the distinction between the

---

[1] For a "taxonomy" of computer pests, see Richard C. Owens, "Turning Worms: Some Thoughts on Liabilities for Spreading Computer Infections" (2004) 3 Canadian Journal of Law and Technology 33 at 34.

two categories is functionally useful and will be employed in the following discussion.

From a legal perspective, the status of malware is less controversial, simply because it is almost always illegal and is easily captured by the tenets of criminal law. Spyware, however, may have legitimate uses as a monitoring or surveillance tool. It may also be unknowingly downloaded onto a user's computer as a non-dangerous data-mining device or, more nefariously, as a means of gaining unauthorized access to personal information for fraudulent purposes. Spyware may be able to record one's keystrokes, passwords, credit card numbers, and may monitor web-surfing activities.

"Adware" applications, which cause advertising banners or pop-ups to be displayed, and which are justified as a means of reducing costs of users and program developers, also often track a user's personal information and pass it on to third parties without the user's consent or knowledge, and consequently usually qualify as spyware.

The United States Center for Democracy & Technology ("CDT") provides the following three categories of applications which are usually described as spyware: (1) key stroke loggers and screen capture utilities which are installed to monitor work habits, observe online behaviour, or capture passwords and other information (often called "snoopware"); (2) "adware" and similar applications that install themselves surreptitiously and track users' behaviours and take advantage of their Internet connection; and (3) legitimate applications that have faulty or weak privacy protection. The CDT states that the first two applications are properly labelled as spyware, and the third is not.[2]

It has been a challenge for the e-commerce industry and the legal community to settle on a definition of spyware for the purpose of developing policies and laws. In a U.S. Federal Trade Commission ("FTC") Staff Report released in 2005, the FTC suggested the following working definition of spyware:

> ... software that aids in gathering information about a person or organization without their knowledge and that may send such information

---

[2]   United States, Center for Democracy and Technology, *Ghosts in Our Machines: Background and Policy Proposals on the "Spyware" Problem — Background and Policy Proposals on the "Spyware" Problem* (Washington D.C.: Center for Democracy and Technology, November, 2003) (hereinafter *CDT Report*).

to another entity without the consumer's consent, or that asserts control over a computer without the consumer's knowledge.[3]

Spyware causes a variety of problems besides the obvious collection and transmission of personal information without the computer user's consent. Spyware applications can change the appearance of Web sites, or change a user's system settings. It often results in significant reductions in computer performance and system stability due to a drain on system resources. Even where personal information is not transmitted, the unauthorized use of a user's computer and Internet connection threatens the integrity of the computer's security. Spyware applications may also create further security vulnerabilities through their automatic downloading capabilities which engage without the knowledge of the user.[4]

II. APPLICATION OF THE *CRIMINAL CODE* TO MALWARE AND SPYWARE

Although the *Criminal Code*[5] does not specifically address malware or spyware, several provisions may be applicable, depending on the circumstances of the particular infection. Notably, the amendments made to the *Criminal Code* that deal with unauthorized use of a computer and mischief in relation to property and data should almost always capture the intentional infection of computers with malware.

A.   Section 342.1: Unauthorized Use of a Computer

The unauthorized access to a computer system is addressed in s. 342.1(1):

342.1(1) Every one who, fraudulently and without colour of right,

(a) obtains, directly or indirectly, any computer service,

---

3   United States, Federal Trade Commission, *Staff Report, Monitoring Software on Your PC: Spyware, Adware and Other Software* (Federal Trade Commission, March, 2005) at 4 (hereinafter *FTC Staff Report*).
4   United States, Center for Democracy and Technology, *Ghosts in Our Machines: Background and Policy Proposals on the "Spyware" Problem — Background and Policy Proposals on the "Spyware" Problem* (Washington D.C.: Center for Democracy and Technology, November, 2005), at 3.
5   R.S.C. 1985, c. C-46.

(*b*) by means of an electro-magnetic, acoustic, mechanical or other device, intercepts or causes to be intercepted, directly or indirectly, any function of a computer system,

(*c*) uses or causes to be used, directly or indirectly, a computer system with intent to commit an offence under paragraph (*a*) or (*b*) or an offence under section 430 [mischief to data] in relation to data or a computer system, or

(*d*) uses, possesses, traffics in or permits another person to have access to a computer password that would enable a person to commit an offence under paragraph (*a*), (*b*) or (*c*)

is guilty of an indictable offence and liable to imprisonment for a term not exceeding ten years, or is guilty of an offence punishable on summary conviction.

"Computer service" is defined broadly to include "data processing and the storage or retrieval of data".[6] For the purposes of this provision "intercept" includes "listen to or record a function of a computer system, or acquire the substance, meaning or purport thereof".[7]

Section 342.1(1) is targeted at unauthorized computer access, or hacking,[8] but because of the broad language employed it would also be useful to prosecute the authors and intentional distributors of malware. For example, it has been suggested that s. 342.1(*a*) and (*c*) would almost always apply to worm infections and those viruses that provide access to computer systems for malevolent purposes.[9] Although there have not been any prosecutions that have used s. 342.1 to combat spyware as of this writing, the potential application of this provision to spyware activities has been suggested by legal commentators.[10]

---

[6]   *Ibid.*, s. 342.1(2).

[7]   *Ibid.*

[8]   See Hackers: a Canadian Police Perspective Part I Prepared by: Criminal Analysis Branch, Criminal Intelligence Directorate, Royal Canadian Mounted Police 2001-05-30 (Web version published 2002-03-14 available online at: <http://www.rcmp.ca/crimint/hackers_e.htm# summary>.

[9]   For a "taxonomy" of computer pests, see Richard C. Owens, "Turning Worms: Some Thoughts on Liabilities for Spreading Computer Infections" (2004) 3 Canadian Journal of Law and Technology 33 at 38.

[10] See, for example, M. Fekete and J. Davidson, "The Growing Threat of Spyware" (2005-06) 6 Internet and E-Commerce Law in Canada. The reasons given by these authors for lack of prosecutions in Canada include a general lack of awareness of the harmful effects of spyware among both law enforcement agencies and legislators; the lack of resources available to the police and prosecutors; minimal media interest in the issue; and the problem of jurisdiction that makes enforcement of Canadian law in the online environment very difficult.

The application of s. 342.1 to spyware will depend on the meaning of "fraudulently", which is discussed below. Presumably, subs. 342.1(*b*) would cover spyware that intercepts computer functions and reports information back to the spyware distributor even if there is no discernable injury to the computer system, or intent to cause other types of computer abuses or harms. Therefore, spyware that is used to gain unauthorized access to personal information, such as passwords or credit card and personal identification numbers, would likely be captured by s. 342.1(*b*) and (*c*). It is less likely that someone who employs spyware to observe surfing behaviour for data mining purposes is doing so fraudulently.

Section 380 may address acts of fraud associated with malware or spyware:

> 380(1) Every one who, *by deceit, falsehood or other fraudulent means*, whether or not it is a false pretence within the meaning of this Act, *defrauds* the public or any person, whether ascertained or not, *of any property, money or valuable security or any service,*
>
> (*a*) is guilty of an indictable offence and liable to a term of imprisonment not exceeding fourteen years, where the subject-matter of the offence is a testamentary instrument or the value of the subject-matter of the offence exceeds five thousand dollars; or
>
> (*b*) is guilty
>
> > (i) of an indictable offence and is liable to imprisonment for a term not exceeding two years, or
> >
> > (ii) of an offence punishable on summary conviction,
>
> where the value of the subject-matter of the offence does not exceed five thousand dollars.

(Emphasis added)

The Supreme Court of Canada provided a general definition of both the *actus reus* and the *mens rea* of fraud in *R. v. Théroux*:[11]

> ... the *actus reus* of the offence of fraud will be established by proof of:
>
> 1. the prohibited act, be it an act of deceit, a falsehood or some other fraudulent means; and
>
> 2. deprivation caused by the prohibited act, which may consist in actual loss or the placing of the victim's pecuniary interests at risk.

---

[11]   [1993] S.C.J. No. 42, [1993] 2 S.C.R. 5, at para. 27.

Correspondingly, the *mens rea* of fraud is established by proof of:

1. subjective knowledge of the prohibited act; and

2. subjective knowledge that the prohibited act could have as a consequence the deprivation of another (which deprivation may consist in knowledge that the victim's pecuniary interests are put at risk).

Even where fraudulent means are used to distribute and install spyware within the meaning of this section, it is questionable whether many types of spyware would qualify as having deprived the owner of the computer of "property, money or valuable security or any service" within the meaning of this section.

B.   Section 430(1.1): Mischief in Relation to Data

Interference with data through the use of malware or spyware might also constitute mischief pursuant to s. 430(1.1):

430(1.1) Every one commits mischief who wilfully

(*a*) destroys or alters data;

(*b*) renders data meaningless, useless or ineffective;

(*c*) obstructs, interrupts or interferes with the lawful use of data; or

(*d*) obstructs, interrupts or interferes with any person in the lawful use of data or denies access to data to any person who is entitled to access thereto.

Malware that produces any of the above effects would be captured by s. 430(1.1). The slowing of computer systems due to infection by malware might also be considered an interruption or interference with data[12] or the interference in use of computer equipment pursuant to s. 430(1), the general mischief to property provision.[13] Similarly, s. 430(1)

---

[12]   Richard C. Owens, "Turning Worms: Some Thoughts on Liabilities for Spreading Computer Infections" (2004) 3 Canadian Journal of Law and Technology 33 at 38.

[13]   Section 430(1):

Every one commits mischief who wilfully

(*a*) destroys or damages property;

(*b*) renders property dangerous, useless, inoperative or ineffective;

(*c*) obstructs, interrupts or interferes with the lawful use, enjoyment or operation of property; or

(*d*) obstructs, interrupts or interferes with any person in the lawful use, enjoyment or operation of property.

may apply where spyware is wilfully installed and interferes with the user's enjoyment or operation of the computer equipment. A common complaint of even the most "harmless" spyware or adware is that it slows down computer performance.

C.   Application of the *Criminal Code* Generally

Other miscellaneous provisions of the *Criminal Code* may apply to certain types of malware depending on the circumstances surrounding a computer's infection. For example, disguised malware contained within an e-mail from a "friendly" sender could constitute forgery.[14]

Although the *Criminal Code* captures a significant portion of malware and spyware activity, the practicality of enforcement is a major problem. Prosecutions are rare because of the difficulty and costs associated with tracing the origins of malware.[15] The Canadian Task Force on Spam, Working Group on Legislation and Enforcement made the following comments with respect to the limitations of applying these *Criminal Code* provisions to spyware:

> Spyware, keylogging and botnets are emerging as very serious perils in Internet usage, and are dangers to the Internet as a critical commercial infrastructure. While there are provisions in the *Criminal Code* that may address certain aspects of these activities, enforcement challenges are such that the *Criminal Code* is an inefficient vehicle for fully addressing the issue. A general provision dealing with consent and user control, carefully worded, could provide a much-needed new tool for capturing these surreptitious activities.[16]

III.   APPLICATION OF *PIPEDA* TO SPYWARE

It seems likely that Canada's federal privacy legislation, the *Personal Information Protection and Electronic Documents Act* ("*PIPEDA*"),[17] and

---

[14]   *Criminal Code*, R.S.C. 1985, c. C-46, s. 366.

[15]   For a "taxonomy" of computer pests, see Richard C. Owens, "Turning Worms: Some Thoughts on Liabilities for Spreading Computer Infections" (2004) 3 Canadian Journal of Law and Technology 33 at 38.

[16]   Canada, Task Force on Spam, *Report of the Working Group on Legislation and Enforcement* (Ottawa: Task Force on Spam, Industry Canada, May, 2005), at Conclusion #4, available online at: <http://e-com.ic.gc.ca/epic/internet/inecic-ceac.nsf/en/h_gv00337e.html> (hereinafter *Spam Report*).

[17]   S.C. 2000, c. 5.

its provincial counterparts would apply to spyware that is employed in a commercial setting, although as of this writing such application remains to be tested. The absence of a commercial spyware case in Canada to date has been attributed to a general lack of awareness and media attention in Canada as compared with the United States, a lack of resources, and the problem of lack of jurisdiction, which is inherent to the Internet.[18]

PIPEDA will only apply to spyware that is employed in the course of "commercial activities".[19] Most adware companies would clearly be engaged in commercial activities in the course of employing various adware applications. Such spyware that does not provide for adequate notice or consent to the collection, use, or disclosure of personal information would violate s. 7 of *PIPEDA*.

A recent decision of the Alberta Privacy Commissioner under that province's *Freedom of Information and Protection of Privacy Act*[20] indicates that privacy legislation could be used to combat spyware. The case[21] involved a complaint filed by an employee of the Parkland Regional Library because the library had installed keystroke logging software on the employee's computer and had collected data about the employee's computer activities without the employee's knowledge. The Commissioner held that the keystroke data constituted "personal information" under the Act.

However, *PIPEDA* would have its limitations in the spyware context. An expensive and lengthy application to the Federal Court would be necessary to levy a penalty against a spyware distributor. The Commissioner's office does not have order-making powers, so a Federal Court enforcement action is needed to obtain an award of damages. The deterrent value of *PIPEDA* is also limited by the federal privacy commissioner's policy of keeping the identity of targets of complaints confidential.

---

[18] Canada, Task Force on Spam, *Report of the Working Group on Legislation and Enforcement* (Ottawa: Task Force on Spam, Industry Canada, May, 2005), at Conclusion #4, available online at: <http://e-com.ic.gc.ca/epic/internet/inecic-ceac.nsf/en/h_gv00337e.html> (hereinafter *Spam Report*) at 4.

[19] S.C. 2000, c. 5, s. 4(1):

This part applies to every organization in respect of personal information that (*a*) the organization collects, uses or discloses in the course of commercial activities; or (*b*) is about an employee of the organization and that the organization collects or uses or discloses in connection with the operation of a federal work undertaken or business.

[20] R.S.A. 2000, c. F-25.

[21] Alberta Office of the Information and Privacy Commissioner, Order F2005-003 (June 24, 2005).

IV. APPLICATION OF THE *COMPETITION ACT* TO SPYWARE

As indicated in the discussion in Chapter 2, the prohibitions in s. 52(1) of the *Competition Act*[22] will apply, in the opinion of the Competition Bureau, to representations made on the Internet. Section 52(1) states:

> 52(1) No person shall, for the purpose of promoting, directly or indirectly, the supply or use of a product or for the purpose of promoting, directly or indirectly, any business interest, by any means whatever, knowingly or recklessly make a representation to the public that is false or misleading in a material respect.

Section 52(1) could cover misleading representations made by many types of spyware distributors who, for example, do not disclose that software or adware contains spyware, do not fully disclose the software's spyware functions, or mislead consumers on the ability to uninstall the spyware. This provision is similar to the "unfair and deceptive acts or practices" provisions in the United States *Federal Trade Commission Act*[23] which are just beginning to be employed against spyware in the United States.

Besides the criminal penalties imposed for violating the *Competition Act*, an individual can also sue to recover from the person who engaged in the conduct an amount equal to the loss or damage proved to have been suffered by him in a civil cause of action for a violation of s. 52(1).[24]

The deceptive marketing provisions[25] in Part VII.I of the *Competition Act*, which consider representations that are misleading in a material respect to be "reviewable conduct" that can result in administrative sanctions or orders, may also be applied to spyware distributors that fail to make adequate disclosure to or mislead consumers in circumstances such as those described above.

---

[22] R.S.C. 1985, c. C-34.
[23] 15 U.S.C. §§ 41-51.
[24] R.S.C. 1985, c. C-34, s. 36.
[25] See the discussion on the application of Part VII.I to consumer protection generally in Chapter 2.

V. LEGISLATIVE REFORM

Canada is only in the preliminary stages of addressing the issue of spyware. The Electronic Commerce Branch of Industry Canada is in the initial stages of designing a policy framework to address spyware and other issues that affect users' confidence in the Internet.

The Office of Consumer Affairs of Industry Canada has granted funds to the Public Interest Advocacy Centre ("PIAC") to study spyware in Canada. The study will examine the categories, risks and functions of spyware, and will survey Canadians on their awareness of spyware. The project will also probe "the use of personal information collected from spyware and whether the collection, use or disclosure of this information violates computer users' rights under the *PIPEDA* and similar provincial legislation".[26]

The Report of the Canadian Task Force on Spam recommends that the federal government "establish in law a clear set of rules to prohibit spam and other emerging threats to the safety and security of the Internet … by enacting new legislation and amending existing legislation as required".[27] However, the recommendations for legislative reform only address spam-related and phishing activities. In the opinion of one author:

> Industry Canada's action plan for spam provides a model for how the federal government can orchestrate a coordinated approach to fighting spyware. Doing nothing cannot be viewed as an option. The prevalence of spyware, and its harmful effects, dictate that the government take a leadership role in implementing a multi-faceted strategy for tackling what has become a significant threat to the privacy and productivity of Canadians.[28]

---

[26] See Public Interest Advocacy Centre (PIAC) "Project Summaries" online: <http://strategis.ic.gc.ca/epic/internet/inoca-bc.nsf/en/ca02076e.html>.

[27] Canada, Task Force on Spam, *Report of the Working Group on Legislation and Enforcement* (Ottawa: Task Force on Spam, Industry Canada, May, 2005), at Conclusion #4, available online at: <http://e-com.ic.gc.ca/epic/internet/inecic-ceac.nsf/en/h_gv00337e.html> (hereinafter *Spam Report*) at 3.

[28] M. Fekete and J. Davidson, "The Growing Threat of Spyware" (2005) 6:1 Internet and E-Commerce Law in Canada at 4.

Reform in the United States has progressed more quickly.[29] Two federal spyware bills have been approved by the U.S. House and are currently being considered by the U.S. Senate. The *Internet Spyware (I-SPY) Prevention Act of 2005*[30] would prohibit the intentional access of a protected computer (a computer exclusively for the use of a financial institution or the U.S. government, or a computer used in interstate or foreign commerce or communication) without authorization by causing a computer program or code to be copied onto the protected computer, and intentionally using that program or code: (1) in furtherance of another Federal criminal offence; (2) to obtain or transmit personal information (including a Social Security number or other government-issued identification number, a bank or credit card number, or an associated password or access code) with intent to defraud or injure a person or cause damage to a protected computer; or (3) to impair the security protection of that computer.[31]

The second Bill, entitled the *Securely Protect Yourself Against Cyber Trespass (Spy Act)*,[32] pertains primarily to adware and would create new unfair and deceptive acts and practices to be enforced by the Federal

---

[29] Many states are currently considering adopting specific spyware legislation. See for example: Alabama's *Consumer Protection Against Spyware Act*, S.B.122; Alaska's *Spyware and Unsolicited Internet Advertising*, S.B.140; Delaware's *Spyware Protection Act*, S.B.124; Florida's *Computer Fraud*, S.B.2162; Illinois's *Spyware Prevention Initiative Act*, H.B.0380; Indiana's *Computer Spyware*, H.B.1714; Kansas' *Computer Protection Against Spyware Act*, H.B.2343; Maryland's *Unauthorized Consumer Software Act*, S.B.492, S.B.801, H.B.945, and H.B.780; Massachusetts' *Prohibiting Spyware*, S.273, *Spyware Control Act*, S.286; and *Consumer Protection Against Spyware Act*, H.B.1444; Michigan's *Spyware Control Act*, S.B.151; Missouri's *Consumer Protection Against Spyware Act*, H.B.902; Nebraska's *Consumer Protection Against Computer Spyware Act*, L.B.316; New Hampshire's *Regulating the Use of Computer Spyware*, H.B.47; New York's *Unlawful Use of Spyware and Malware*, A.00549, *Unlawful Dissemination of Spyware*, S.00186 and A.02682, and S.07141; Oregon's *Spyware*, H.B.2302; Pennsylvania's *Misuse of Adware or Spyware*, H.B.574; Rhode Island's *Software Fraud*, H.B.6211; Tennessee's *Internet Spyware Control Act*, H.B.1742 and S.B.2069; Texas' *Collection and Transmission of Certain Information by Computer*, S.B.327, *Consumer Protection Against Computer Spyware Act*, H.B.1351, and *Consumer Protection Against Computer Spyware Act*, H.B.1430 and S.B.958; Virginia's *Prohibited Software and Actions*, H.B.1729, and *Invasive Technologies*, H.B. 1304; West Virginia's *Spyware Disclosure*, H.B.3246; California's *Computer Adware and Spyware*, A.B.2787; and Iowa's Senate File 2200; Michigan's, S.B.1315.

[30] H.R. 744, 109th Cong. (1st Sess. 2005) (status available online: <http://thomas.loc.gov/home/thomas.html>).

[31] *Ibid.* at § 3. Note that § 4 provides for the allocation of resources for enforcement. It provides for the appropriation of "the sum of $10,000,000 to the Attorney General for prosecutions needed to discourage the use of spyware and phishing.

[32] H.R. 29, 109th Cong. (1st Sess. 2005) (status available online: <http://thomas.loc.gov/home/thomas.html>).

Trade Commission.[33] The *Spy Act* would make it unlawful for any person who is not the owner or authorized user of a protected computer to engage in unfair or deceptive acts or practices in connection with specified conduct. Such practices would include taking unsolicited control of the computer, modifying computer settings, collecting personally identifiable information with a keystroke logger, inducing the owner or authorized user to disclose personally identifiable information by using a misleading Web page, and inducing the unsolicited installation of computer software.[34]

The Act would provide an opt-in requirement for adware, making it unlawful for a person to transmit to a protected computer or execute any program that collects personally identifiable information and uses that information to send advertising, unless such program provides notice required by the Act before execution of any of the program's collection functions.[35] Failure to abide by the Act could provide for significant penalties of up to $3,000,000 for the unfair and deceptive acts or practices outlined above, and up to $1,000,000 for an adware notice violation.[36]

Tackling spyware through legislation will not be a panacea, and even the Federal Trade Commission has concerns that legislation will not be as effective as technological solutions.[37] It is also possible that strict anti-spyware legislation that is drafted too broadly could capture legitimate business practices, such as the provision of automatic software updates.

The *CDT Report* expresses the view that it would be very difficult to craft a definition of "spyware" that is precise enough for legislation. Instead, the CDT recommends using a combination of more general privacy legislation articulating basic privacy standards to which all programs should be held, and legislation addressing spyware as a trespass problem.[38]

---

[33] 15 U.S.C. § 57a. A violation of any provision of the Act or of a regulation issued under the Act would be treated as an unfair or deceptive act or practice violating a rule under § 18 of the *Federal Trade Commission Act*.

[34] H.R. 29, 109th Cong. (1st Sess. 2005) (status available online: <http://thomas.loc.gov/home/thomas.html>) at § 2.

[35] *Ibid.*, at § 3.

[36] *Ibid.*, at § 4(b).

[37] W. Jackson, "FTC: Technology, not legislation, needed to fight spyware" *GNC.com* (5 November, 2004), online: <http://www.gcn.com/vol1_no1/daily-updates/27845-1.html>.

[38] United States, Center for Democracy and Technology, *Ghosts in Our Machines: Background and Policy Proposals on the "Spyware" Problem — Background and Policy Proposals on the "Spyware" Problem* (Washington D.C.: Center for Democracy and Technology, November, 2003) (hereinafter *CDT Report*), at 12.

What emerges from the American attempts to combat spyware legislatively, and Canada's tentative foray into studying the problem, is that a coordination of efforts encompassing technological, legislative, and consumer awareness measures will likely be necessary. One of the tools currently at the disposal of both business and consumers is the application of established common law principles to this novel issue, which is the topic addressed in the following section.

VI. USING THE COMMON LAW TO BATTLE SPYWARE AND MALWARE

A. Trespass to Chattels

The U.S. Courts have recently been called upon to consider the application of the tort of trespass to chattels in circumstances involving the downloading of software to computers. To make a successful claim for the tort of trespass to chattels under Canadian law, a claimant must prove on a balance of probabilities that the defendant has committed an act of direct interference with the claimant's tangible personal property without any lawful justification.[39] The United States Restatement (Second) of Torts, §217(b) defines the tort with essentially the same elements.

Courts in Canada have yet to address the issue of trespass to chattels in any online context. United States ISPs have had initial success employing the tort of trespass in targeting spam. For example, in the leading case *Compuserve Inc. v. Cyber Promotions*[40] the plaintiff ISP was granted a preliminary injunction against a spammer that generated massive amounts of unsolicited commercial e-mail, which placed a significant burden on the plaintiff's computing equipment, because such circumstances could sustain a viable claim in trespass. The court recognized that a trespass to chattels may be committed by "intentionally using or intermeddling with the chattel in possession of another" and that "electronic signals generated and sent by a computer had been held to be sufficiently physically tangible to support a trespass cause of action".[41] CompuServe's claims that the spam caused harm to its business reputation and goodwill was sufficient to allow the claim in trespass to go forward.[42]

---

[39] Philip H. Osborne, *The Law of Torts*, 2nd. ed. (Toronto: Irwin, 2003), at 274-75.
[40] 962 F. Supp. 1015, 1997 U.S. Dist. LEXIS 1997, 25 Media L. Rep 1545 (S.D. Ohio 1997).
[41] *Ibid.*, at 1021.
[42] Cases that have applied similar reasoning include: *Ferguson v. Friendfinders, Inc.*, 94 Cal.App. 4th 1255, 1267 [115 Cal. Rptr. 2d 258] (2002); *Hotmail Corp. v. Van$ Money Pie,*

Other American cases have been more cautious is applying the tort of trespass to electronic communications, indicating that trespass will not apply to such communications unless they manifestly damage or impair the functioning of the recipient's computer system.[43] However, it should be noted that in Canada intentional torts, including trespass to chattels, are usually actional *per se*, and do not require proof of damage.[44]

Several American cases have also held that unauthorized robotic data collection (also known as the use of "web bots" or "spiders") from a company's publicly accessible web site constitutes trespass. In *eBay v. Bidder's Edge*,[45] the defendant accessed the eBay web site aproximately 100,000 times per day requesting information to aid the operation of its own auction site. In granting a preliminary injunction, the court found that eBay had shown a strong likelihood of prevailing on the merits of a trespass claim, as eBay was likely to be able to demonstrate that the defendant's activities diminished the quality or value of eBay's computer systems:

> Although eBay does not claim that this consumption has led to any physical damage to eBay's computer system, nor does eBay provide any evidence to support the claim that it may have lost revenues or customers based on this use, eBay's claim is that BE's use is appropriating eBay's personal property by using valuable bandwidth and capacity, and necessarily compromising eBay's ability to use that capacity for its own purposes.[46]
>
> ...
>
> If BE's activity is allowed to continue unchecked, it would encourage other auction aggregators to engage in similar recursive searching of the eBay system such that eBay would suffer irreparable harm from reduced system performance, system unavailability, or data losses.[47]

The principles of trespass law that have been applied to combat spam and robotic data collection could similarly be used to target spyware. In 2005, a federal U.S. District Court in Illinois held that a claim of trespass to personal property could be asserted by an individual computer user who alleges unauthorized electronic contact with the user's

---

Inc. 1998 WL 388389 (N.D. Cal., 1998, No. C 98-20064 JW), at 7; *America Online, Inc. v. IMS*, 24 F. Supp. 2d 548, at 550-51 (E.D. Va. 1998); *America Online, Inc. v. LCGM, Inc.*, 46 F. Supp. 2d 444, at 451-52 (E.D.Va. 1998).

[43]   See, for example, *Intel Corporation v. Hamidi*, 30 Cal. 4th 1342 (Cal. Sup. Ct. 2003).

[44]   G.J.L. Fridman, *The Law of Torts in Canada* (Toronto: Carswell, 1989), at 7.

[45]   *eBay, Inc. v. Bidder's Edge, Inc.*, 100 F. Supp. 2d 1058 (N.D. Cal. 2000).

[46]   *Ibid.*, at 1071.

[47]   *Ibid.*, at 1066.

computer system by means of spyware. In *Sotelo v. DirectRevenue, LLC*[48] the defendant installed spyware on thousands of computers, which tracked web browsing behaviour of computer users and then used that information to send targeted "pop-up" advertising to those computers. The court made note of the fact that the antiquated tort of "trespass to property" had re-emerged as a useful cause of action in several Internet-related cases. The court was satisfied that the tort could be applied to spyware activities, and consequently denied the defendant's motion to dismiss the action.

In another recent motion before a United States District Court in California,[49] a company that allegedly distributed spyware and adware to track online users' browsing habits was unsuccessful in its attempt to dismiss the plaintiffs' trespass to chattels claim. The court found that the allegations, which included reducing the efficiency of the plaintiffs' computer system and damaging existing software, were sufficient to support an action for trespass to chattels.

The Sony Rootkit controversy, in which technological protection measures ("TPMs") designed to protect Sony's copyrights in music CDs hid their existence by integrating into a computer's operating system, also raises the possibility of applying trespass to chattels to non-consensual installation of TPMs. The TPMs were downloaded from purchased CDs, and resulted in security vulnerabilities to those computers onto which the CDs were installed. A class action settlement of the case (which included a pleading of trespass to chattels) has been reached in the United States,[50] although at the time of this writing class actions remain extant in Canada.[51]

It should be noted that the reasoning applied in the trespass to chattels cases in the United States has been criticized for interfering with the optimum functioning of the Internet. At least one Canadian writer argues that such an approach perpetuates the proliferation of exclusive property rights in the online environment, which was designed to operate as a "commons".[52] These critics castigate the courts for effectively creating new common law property rights that are transforming the

---

[48] 384 F.Supp.2d 1219 (N.D. Ill. 2005).

[49] *Thomas Kerrins v. Intermix Media,* No. 2:05-cv-05408-RGK-SS (C.D. Cal. 2006).

[50] Settlement motion available online: <http://www.sunbelt-software.com/ihs/alex/sonysettleme 23423423434nt.pdf>.

[51] See the web sites of L'Union des consommateurs: <http://www.consommateur.qc.ca/union/>; and PrivacyInfo.ca: <http://www.privacyinfo.ca/>.

[52] See W.A. Adams, "There Is No There There: *Intel Corp. v. Hamidi* and the Creation of New Common Law Property Rights Online" (2004) 40 Can. Bus. L. J. 87.

Internet into a series of private property transactions.[53] In response to such criticism one might argue that the proliferation of harmful spyware, malware, and spam renders any notion of a happy, inclusive, open-access community an illusion. In the absence of specific legislative protections, the courts should be encouraged to protect consumers by applying common law principles to prevent the networked commons, in which consumers participate, from becoming dysfunctional.

B.   Tort of Invasion of Privacy

The practical limitations of the application of the *PIPEDA* to spyware have been discussed. There are also limitations to approaching the problem of invasion of privacy via the common law. Historically, Canada has not recognized a common law tort of "invasion of privacy", although there is some indication that the impact of technological innovations on privacy may herald a greater awareness of privacy rights by the courts. The case law is inconsistent, but a significant number of courts in Canada have indicated that they are likely headed in that direction.[54]

In 2006 the Ontario Superior Court addressed the fundamental issue of whether Ontario law recognizes the tort of invasion of privacy. The case, *Somwar v. McDonald's Restaurants Canada Ltd.*,[55] involved a suit by an employee over a credit bureau check on the employee by his employer, without the employee's consent. The employer sought an order dismissing the plaintiff's action on the ground that the statement of claim disclosed no reasonable cause of action.

The court concluded that it was not settled law in Ontario that there is no tort of invasion of privacy, and in fact felt that such a tort should at last be recognized:

> Even if the plaintiff's claim for invasion of privacy were classified as "novel" (which, in any event, is not a proper basis for dismissing it) the foregoing analysis leads me to conclude that the time has come to

---

[53]   *Ibid.*, at 106; see also L. Quilter, "The Continuing Expansion of Cyberspace Trespass to Chattels" (2002) 17 Berkley Tech. L.J. 421.

[54]   See for example: *Ontario (Attorney General) v. Dieleman*, [1994] O.J. No. 1864, 117 D.L.R. (4th) 449 (Gen. Div.) where the court concluded after a review of the case law prior to 1994, that one could not speak with confidence of a Canadian tort of invasion of privacy; but in 1996 an Ontario court held an intentional invasion of privacy was committed when an individual focused a surveillance camera on a neighbour's backyard (*Lipiec v. Borsa*, [1996] O.J. No. 3819, 31 C.C.L.T. (2d) 294 (Gen. Div.)).

[55]   [2006] O.J. No. 64 (S.C.J.).

recognize invasion of privacy as a tort in its own right. It therefore follows that it is neither plain nor obvious that the plaintiff's action cannot succeed on the basis that he has not pleaded a reasonable cause of action.[56]

As well, several provinces have adopted privacy legislation[57] that establishes the right to file an action for breach of privacy against any person who knowingly and wrongfully violates the privacy of another person. Quebec's *Civil Code* also establishes a right to privacy.[58]

Although it is yet uncertain whether invasion of privacy could be successfully employed in Canada to combat spyware, commentators in the United States have indicated that the better-developed invasion of privacy tort in that jurisdiction could be applied to spyware that reaches a level of serious or unreasonable intrusion:

> If the computer invader does not have a right to access the computer to install the software, the court should find that the computer user has a high expectation of privacy. If the court finds there is a legitimate business interest or consent, it could rule the claim is invalid. The court will look at the factors surrounding the alleged invasion, including how the user gained access to the computer to install the software, to determine if it reaches the level of a serious or substantial intrusion.
>
> ...
>
> A user does not have the ability to deny access to his privacy when he does not know there is software that captures his deleted thoughts. A court could find an unreasonable intrusion by using the balancing test that weighs the seriousness of the offense against the importance of the public interest.[59]

VII. CONSUMER AWARENESS

As with identity theft, legal protections must be supplemented with consumer awareness in order to effectively tackle spyware and malware problems. Several consumer education Web sites aim to assist Internet

---

[56] *Ibid.*, at para. 31.

[57] See, for example, the Privacy Acts of British Columbia, Newfoundland, Saskatchewan, and Manitoba:, R.S.B.C.1996, c. 373, s. 1; R.S.N.L. 1990, c. P-22, s. 3; R.S.S. 1978, c. P-24, s. 2; C.C.S.M. c. P125, s. 2.

[58] Articles 35-41 C.C.Q.

[59] J. H. McNulty. "Who Is Watching Your Keystrokes? An Analysis of M.G.L. ch. 214 § 1B, Right to Privacy and Its Effectiveness Against Computer Surveillance" (2003) 2:1 Jour. High Tech Law 67 at 83, online: <http://www.jhtl.org/>.

users in preventing the downloading of spyware and malware. For example, the Public Interest Advocacy Centre, a non-profit organization that provides legal and research services on behalf of consumer interests, contains information about privacy and electronic commerce.[60] The Canadian Internet Policy and Public Interest Clinic, an Ottawa-based legal clinic, provides a detailed web page on spyware, including technological applications for detection and removal, and information on Canadian laws that are applicable to spyware.[61] The Anti-Spyware Coalition, comprised of anti-spyware vendors, Internet service providers, technology companies, and consumer groups, provides consumer information on spyware, including a vendor dispute resolution process and safety tips for users.[62]

A well-informed consumer can take the necessary precautions to avoid the effects of the most pernicious forms of spyware. Knowledge of the extent of the problem, the legal mechanisms available to tackle it, and the gaps in existing law is vital if one is to challenge the status quo online. Consumer activism has experienced a resurgence in response to new online threats and annoyances. For example, proceedings under class actions legislation have brought the Sony Rootkit controversy to the attention of the media and the public.[63] Consumer activism is also noticed by politicians and officials charged with law enforcement, who may take action in response to vocal consumer concerns.[64]

---

[60] Online: <www.piac.ca>.

[61] Online: <http://www.cippic.ca/en/faqs-resources/spyware/>.

[62] Online: <http://www.antispywarecoalition.org>.

[63] See the web sites of L'Union des consommateurs: <http://www.consommateur.qc.ca/union/>; and PrivacyInfo.ca: <http://www.privacyinfo.ca/>.

[64] For example, the Attorney General of New York has filed a lawsuit against an Internet spyware company, seeking a court order enjoining the company from secretly installing spyware or sending ads through already-installed spyware. Once downloaded, the particular spyware is extremely difficult for users to detect and remove. See Office of the New York State Attorney General, online: <http://www.oag.state.ny.us/press/2006/apr/apr04a_06.html>.

INDEX

Cancellation of internet sales contract.
See also **Internet Sales Contract Harmonization Template** and **Template concordance with provincial legislation**
- consumers able to cancel online agreement in specific circumstances, 26-27, 40-41
- "cooling-off" period, 26-27
- court able to make appropriate order, 27, 41
- effect of cancellation, 42
- notice of cancellation, 27, 41-42
- refund, recovery of, 27, 43
- responsibilities of consumer, 27, 42-43
- responsibilities of supplier, 27, 42, 43
- Template concordance with provincial legislation, 81-110
- variation in consumer's right of cancellation, 27-28

Click-wrap agreements. *See also* **Electronic Contract**
- "electronically execute" agreement, 5-6
- • court's lack of concern for consequences, 6
- • forum selection clauses possibly unconscionable, 6
- • notion of unconscionability ignored due to need for commercial certainty, 6
- • portion of agreement viewed at any one time, 5-6
- notice of amendment permitted by posting notice on Web site, 6-8
- • *Consumer Protection Act, 2002* (CPA, 2002) preventing unilateral changes, 7-8
- • disclaimer clauses limiting liability not enforceable in online trading, 8
- • mandatory arbitration clause added with no other notice, 6-8
- • • CPA, 2002 preventing unilateral changes, 7

- • • such arbitration clause unconscionable in United States, 7
- • • subscribers expected to review Web site for amendment to user agreement, 7
- • • user agreement not improvident, 7
- online consumer contracts being contracts of adhesion, 5

Competition Act
- deceptive marketing, 34
- • administrative procedures, 34
- • • "reviewable conduct", 34
- • • defence for person merely disseminating or distributing representation, 34
- • • • defence available where not having decision-making authority or content control, 34
- • • misleading representations, 34
- deceptive notice of winning prize, 34-35
- • • offence under Act, 35
- • • • sentencing considerations, 35
- • • prohibition against sending electronic mail to give impression of winning, 34-35
- • • provision useful in targeting spam, 35
- deceptive telemarketing, 35
- disclaimers improperly placed amounting to misleading representations, 35
- • Competition Bureau's views on scrolling, hyperlinks and "pop-ups", 35
- • disclaimers to be prominently and conspicuously placed, 35
- false or misleading representations on Internet, 32-34
- • intermediaries not normally considered persons who caused representations, 33
- • • whether control over content, 33
- • offence under Act, 32-33

Competition Act — cont'd
- • representation from Canada, 33-34
- • representation from outside Canada, 33
- • representation to public, 32-33
- • whether "real and substantial connection" between offence and Canada, 34
- generally, 32
- phishing, 144
- prevention of identity theft, 148
- specific products, 35-36
- spyware, 157
- • deceptive marketing provisions, 157
- • misleading representations by spyware distributors, 157
- • remedies under Act, 157
- • "unfair and deceptive acts or practices" provisions in U.S., 15
- unfair trade practices under provincial legislation, 35

Credit card charges, reversal of
- consumer able to request credit card issuer to cancel credit card charge, 28, 43
- • request to contain prescribed information, 43-44
- • where refund not made within stipulated 15-day period, 28
- credit card issuer required to cancel credit card charge, 28-29, 44
- • American Fair Credit Billing Act deviating from Template requirements, 29
- • contravention of duties constituting offence, 28-29
- • Ontario giving discretion to credit card issuers, 29
- • Template providing standard legal course of action, 29
- Template concordance with provincial legislation, 110-122

Criminal Code. See also **Security of personal information**
- identity theft, provisions applicable to, 126-128
- • credit card offences, 127
- • false pretences, 127

- • forgery, 127-128
- • fraudulent conduct, 127
- • personation, 127
- phishing, 128, 144-146
- • computer system, unauthorized access to, 145
- • • "computer system" defined, 145
- • false messages with intent to injure, 144-145
- • fraud, form of, 144
- • limited in effectiveness, 145
- malware and spyware, 151-155
- • generally, 155
- • • Canadian Task Force on Spam, 155
- • • practicality of enforcement being major problem, 155
- • mischief in relation to data, 154-155
- • • *Code* provision, 154
- • • malware producing prescribed effects, 154
- • • spyware interfering with user's enjoyment or operation, 154-155
- • unauthorized use of computer: s. 342.1, 151-154
- • • *Code* provision, 151-152
- • • "computer service" defined, 152
- • • fraud associated with malware or spyware, where, 153-154
- • • prosecution of authors and intentional distributors of malware, useful for, 152
- • • spyware intercepting computer functions and reporting back information, 153
- Task Force on Spam Background Report, 145-146

Definitions
- "consumer", 37, 46-47
- • Alberta, 46
- • British Columbia, 46
- • Manitoba, 47
- • Nova Scotia, 47
- • Ontario, 47
- • Template, 37, 46
- "consumer transaction", 47-48
- • Alberta, 47
- • British Columbia, 47-48
- • Manitoba, 48

Definitions — *cont'd*
- • Nova Scotia, 48
- • Ontario, 47
- • Template, 47
- "goods", 48-49
- • Alberta, 48
- • British Columbia, 49
- • Manitoba, 49
- • Nova Scotia, 49
- • Ontario, 49
- • Template, 48
- "internet", 49
- • Alberta, 49
- • British Columbia, 49
- • Manitoba, 49
- • Nova Scotia, 49
- • Ontario, 49
- • Template, 49
- "internet sales contract", 37, 50
- • Alberta, 50
- • British Columbia, 50
- • Manitoba, 50
- • Nova Scotia, 50
- • Ontario, 50
- • Template, 37, 50
- "services", 51-52
- • Alberta, 51
- • British Columbia, 51
- • Manitoba, 51-52
- • Nova Scotia, 52
- • Ontario, 52
- • Template, 51
- "supplier", 37, 52-53
- • Alberta, 52
- • British Columbia, 52-53
- • Manitoba, 53
- • Nova Scotia, 53
- • Ontario, 53
- • Template, 37, 52
- Template variations, 53-55
- • British Columbia, 53-54
- • • "distance sales contract", 53
- • • "future performance contract", 53-54
- • Manitoba, 54-55
- • • "buyer", 47, 54
- • • "retail hire-purchase, 54-55
- • • "retail sale", 55
- • • "seller", 53, 54

- • *Uniform Electronic Commerce Act (UECA)*, 9
- • • "electronic", 9
- • • "electronic signature", 9
- • • "Government", 9

Disclosure of information. *See also* **Internet Sales Contract Harmonization Template** and **Template concordance with provincial legislation**
- copy of contract in writing or in electronic format, 24-25, 39-40
- • means of providing copy, 40
- • Template concordance with provincial legislation, 74-81
- failure to disclose providing consumer with right of cancellation, 23-24
- prominently displayed in clear and comprehensive manner, 24
- standard information, 24, 37-38
- supplier's e-mail address, 24
- Template concordance with provincial legislation, 58-73

Electronic contract
- formation of online contracts, 1-4
- • acceptance, 3-4
- • • communication of acceptance usually by electronic mail, 4
- • • electronic document *sent* or *received*, when, 3-4
- • • instantaneous communications not subject to mailbox rule, 4
- • • mailbox rule not stipulated under UECA, 4
- • • mechanics of acceptance stipulated on Web sites, 4
- • • when acceptance occurring with online communications, 4
- • offer or invitation to treat, 3
- • *Uniform Electronic Commerce Act (UECA)* generally, 1-3, 15-16
- • • "click-wrap" contracts being enforceable in Canada, 2-3
- • • electronic agents resulting in binding contracts, interaction with, 3
- • • electronic equivalence of written and electronic communications, 1-2

Electronic contract — *cont'd*
- • • rules governing formation of electronic contracts, 1-2
- • • standards relating to contracting over open electronic networks, 1
- • introduction, 1
- • • online environment, contractual principles relating to, 1
- • • private law of contract applying, 1
- • notice of terms, 5-8
- • • browse-wrap agreements, 8
- • • click-wrap agreements, 5-8
- • • • "electronically execute" agreement, 5-6
- • • • notice of amendment permitted by posting notice on Web site, 6-8
- • online consumer contracts being contracts of adhesion, 5

Hercules Management Ltd. v. Ernst & Young
- • auditors, tortious liability of, 137-139
- • • "expectation gap" faced by accounting profession, 137
- • • foreseeability of reliance and harm not suffice to impose liability, 137
- • • two-part test for determining whether auditors owed duty of care to investors, 138
- • • • policy considerations that might limit or even deny recovery, 138
- • • • "proximity": foreseeability by auditor and reliance by investors, 138
- • • WebTrust seal insulating auditors from liability, 138
- • Web seal providers, liability of, 138-139

History of online consumer protection in Canada
- • Industry Canada commissioning 1998 Report on adequacy of existing legislation, 20-21
- • Internet Sales Contract Harmonization Template, 21
- • • guide in realizing legislative uniformity in various jurisdictions, 21
- • traditional purchaser and consumer protection legislation continuing to apply, 19-20
- • voluntary code of practice, 21
- • • Canadian Code of Practice for Consumer Protection in Electronic Commerce, 21
- • voluntary system of good business practices, 21

Identity theft. *See* **"Phishing"** and **Security of personal information**

Internet Sales Contract Harmonization Template. *See also* **Template concordance with provincial legislation**
- • application of template, 23, 38
- • • "consumer" defined, 23, 37
- • • "internet sales contracts" defined, 23, 37
- • • online purchase of goods and services by consumers, 23
- • cancellation of internet sales contract, 26-28, 40-43
- • • consumers able to cancel online agreement in specific circumstances, 26-27, 40-41
- • • "cooling-off" period, 26, 27
- • • court able to make appropriate order, 27, 41
- • • effect of cancellation, 42
- • • notice of cancellation, 27, 41-42
- • • refund, recovery of, 27, 43
- • • responsibilities of consumer, 27, 42-43
- • • responsibilities of supplier, 27, 42, 43
- • • variation in consumer's right of cancellation, 27-28
- • contract formation, 25-26
- • • Template not addressing mechanics of online contract formation, 25
- • • Template requiring opportunity for consumer to accept or decline online contract, 25
- • • • clicking "I agree" icon, 25
- • • • UECA and provincial legislation having similar requirement, 25-26

Internet Sales Contract Harmonization Template — *cont'd*
- credit card charges, reversal of, 27-29, 43-44
- • consumer able to request credit card issuer to cancel credit card charge, 28, 43
- • • request to contain prescribed information, 43-44
- • • where refund not made within stipulated 15-day period, 28
- • credit card issuer required to cancel credit card charge, 28-29, 44
- • • American *Fair Credit Billing Act* deviating from Template requirements, 29
- • • contravention of duties constituting offence, 28-29
- • • Ontario giving discretion to credit card issuers, 29
- • • Template providing standard legal course of action, 29
- definitions, 37
- • "consumer", 37
- • "internet sales contract", 37
- • "supplier", 37
- disclosure of information, 23-25, 38-40
- • copy of contract in writing or in electronic format, 24-25, 39-40
- • • means of providing copy, 40
- • failure to disclose providing consumer with right of cancellation, 23-24
- • prominently displayed in clear and comprehensive manner, 24
- • standard information, 24, 37-38
- • supplier's e-mail address, 24
- introduction, 22-23
- • five provinces having legislation reflective of Template, 22-23
- • • provincial variations, 22-23
- • four headings of topics, 22
- • new consumer issues not addressed, 22
- • rules relating to online buying and selling, 22
- offence, 44

Invasion of privacy, 164-165. *See also* **Spyware and Malware**

Jurisdictional issues. *See also Competition Act*
- agreement as to applicable law in consumer contract, 31
- • agreement not depriving consumer of protection under home jurisdiction, 31
- • applicable law where no agreement, 31
- Alberta's *Internet Sales Contract Regulation*, 30
- • offer or acceptance made in or sent from Alberta, 30
- • supplier or consumer resident in Alberta, 30
- conflicts of law, 30
- • "jurisdiction of destination" approach, 30
- • "real and substantial connection" to jurisdiction, 30
- forum selection clauses, 6, 30
- • clauses possibly unconscionable, 6
- generally, 29
- "jurisdiction of destination" approach, 30
- • European Union's Brussels Regulation variation of model, 30
- Nova Scotia requiring "real and substantial" connection to province, 30-31
- Uniform Law Conference of Canada proposals, 31-32
- • agreement as to applicable law in consumer contract, 31
- • option of proceedings against vendor in consumer's or vendor's jurisdiction, 31-32

Malware. *See* **Spyware and Malware**

Overview
- disconnect between practical realities and academic attention, xvi
- "distance sale" nature of online purchases, xvi
- Internet expanding notions of consumer protection, xv, xvi

Overview — *cont'd*
- Internet forcing re-conceptualizing of established legal principles, xv
- music downloading as consumer issue, xv-xvi
- • inadequacy of existing copyright legislation, xv
- online consumer lacking practical recourse, xvi
- "phishing" threatening to erode consumer confidence, xv
- privacy and security of personal information being consumer protection issues, xv
- spammers engaging in criminal-like behaviour targeting consumers, xv
- traditional buyer/seller rights and obligations vs. novel issues, xvi

Personal Information Protection and Electronic Documents Act (PIPEDA)
- criticism of *PIPEDA* for lacking strength in protecting privacy, 129-130, 144
- principle possibly supporting duty of care, 133
- phishing, 143-144
- • "address harvesting" by spammers for phishing purposes captured by *PIPEDA*, 143
- • collection and use of personal information requiring consent of individual, 143
- • • exception if information publicly available, 143
- • limited ability in combating phishing, 144
- • • Task Force on Spam Background Report, 144
- • unsolicited commercial bulk e-mail, applying to, 143
- protections relevant to prevention of identity theft, 129
- requirement for adequate safeguards to protect personal information, 131
- requirements under *PIPEDA* working against efforts to verify identity, 129
- spyware, 155-156
- • "commercial activities", 156
- • • adware companies, 156

- • Federal Court proceedings being expensive and lengthy, 156
- • keystroke logging data constituting "personal information", 156
- • spyware employed in commercial setting, 156

Personal information, security of. *See* **Security of personal information**

"Phishing". *See also* **Security of personal information**
- introduction, 141-142
- • activity related to unsolicited e-mail or "spam", 142
- • "pharming" defined, 142
- • "phishing", meaning of, 141-142
- • • e-mail lures used to "fish" for passwords and financial data from Internet users, 42
- • threatening to erode consumer confidence, xv
- • variants of phishing schemes, 142
- legislative reform, 146-147
- • Task Force on Spam Report, 146-147
- • • recommendations relating to phishing, 146-147
- • *Telecommunications Act* amendment, 147
- • • do-not-call list (DNCL) administered by CRTC, 147
- • • do-not-spam equivalent to DNCL, 147
- legislation applicable to phishing, 143-146
- • *Competition Act*, 144
- • *Criminal Code*, 144-146
- • • computer system, unauthorized access to, 145
- • • false messages with intent to injure, 144-145
- • • fraud, form of, 144
- • • limited in effectiveness, 145
- • • Task Force on Spam Background Report, 145-146
- • *PIPEDA*, 143-144
- • • "address harvesting" by spammers for phishing purposes captured by *PIPEDA*, 143

"Phishing" — *cont'd*
- • • collection and use of personal information requiring consent of individual, 143
- • • limited ability in combating phishing, 144
- • • unsolicited commercial bulk e-mail, applying to, 143

Provincial legislation. *See* **Template concordance with provincial legislation**

"Seals" of approval. *See* **Security of personal information**

Security of personal information. *See also* **"Phishing"**
- • common law liability, 133-134
- • • CMC Report suggesting statutory cause of action, 133
- • • consumers forced to argue duty to notify under common or civil law principles, 134
- • • duty of care as analyzed by Supreme Court of Canada, 134
- • • • impediment on law of negligence's ability to adopt to technological relationship, 134
- • • *PIPEDA* principle possibly supporting duty of care, 133
- • • tort law appearing inadequate in protecting consumers, 133
- • consumer reporting legislation, 130-131
- • • consumer rights related to consumer or credit reports, 130
- • • criticism of consumer reporting legislation, 130-131
- • • Nova Scotia *Consumer Reporting Act*, 130
- • • Ontario's *Consumer Reporting Act*, 130
- • criminal laws applicable to identity theft, 126-129
- • • *Criminal Code* provisions applicable, 126-128
- • • • credit card offences, 127
- • • • false pretences, 127
- • • • forgery, 127-128
- • • • fraudulent conduct, 127
- • • • personation, 127
- • • • "phishing", 128
- • • *Employment Insurance Act*, 128
- • • online identity theft not adequately served by criminal legislation, 128
- • • *Vital Statistics Act*, 128-129
- • introduction, 125-126
- • • identity theft as major consumer protection issue, 125
- • • "identity theft" defined, 125
- • • Internet providing medium for criminals to access personal data, 125
- • • victims of identity theft, 125-126
- • legislation and common law protection generally, 126
- • legislative reform, 131-132
- • • Consumer Measures Committee (CMC) Report, 132
- • • • suggested reforms, 132
- • • notification of breach of security, 131
- • • *PIPEDA* requiring adequate safeguards to protect personal information, 131
- • prevention of identity theft, 148
- • • Canadian Bankers Association (CBA) best practices, 148
- • • Competition Bureau's anti-fraud campaign, 148
- • • Consumer Measures Committee (CMC) publications, 148
- • • education and prevention efforts, 148
- • • PhoneBusters anti-fraud call centre, 148
- • privacy and security "seals", legal implications of, 134-141
- • • auditors, tortious liability of, 137-139
- • • • "expectation gap" faced by accounting profession, 137
- • • • foreseeability of reliance and harm not suffice to impose liability, 137
- • • • two-part test for determining whether auditors owed duty of care to investors, 138

Security of personal information —
cont'd
- • • WebTrust seal insulating auditors from liability, 138
- • • auditors vs. Web seal providers: analogy problematic, 139-140
- • • audited statements required under legislation while privacy audit not required, 139
- • • "free-ridership" concern, 139-140
- • • policy considerations not applicable in Web seal context, 140
- • • WebTrust seal providing assurances to third parties of privacy standards, 139
- • common law liability for misrepresentation, 140
- • foreseeability of reliance and harm not suffice to impose liability, 137
- • "free-ridership" concern, 138-140
- • policy considerations possibly vitiating duty of care of Web seal providers, 138-139
- • "proximity" analysis applicable to Web seal providers, 138-139
- • reform suggestions, 140-141
- • • aggressive monitoring program for non-compliance, 140
- • • privacy law being consumer's primary protection, 140-141
- • • trust mark, adoption of, 140
- • • Web seals playing valuable educational role in promoting privacy awareness, 141
- • "seals" of approval on Web sites. 135
- • self-regulation model, 134-135
- • Toysmat case, 136
- • • TRUSTe seal of assurance re privacy of personal information, 136
- • • Web certifiers serving as "watchdogs" at best, 136
- • TRUSTe "trustmark" certifying compliance with stated privacy policies, 135-137
- • Web seal assurances not preventing serious breaches of security, 136

- • • seal providers failing to monitor Web site businesses granted seal, 136
- • Web seals creating dangerous illusion of privacy protection, 136-137
- • • purchase of personal customer information from company with TRUSTEe seal, 137
- • "WebTrust" seal provided by Canadian Institute of Chartered Accountants, 135, 137-139
- • • "expectation gap" faced by accounting profession, 137
- • • WebTrust seal insulating auditors from liability, 138
- • • whether seal providing online consumers with high level of assurance of privacy, 137
- • privacy legislation, 129-130
- • *Personal Information Protection and Electronic Documents Act (PIPEDA)*, 129-130
- • • criticism of *PIPEDA*, 129-130
- • • protections relevant to prevention of identity theft, 129
- • • requirements under *PIPEDA* working against efforts to verify identity, 129

Spam. *See* **"Phishing"** and **Spyware and Malware**

Spyware and Malware
- • common law used to combat spyware and malware, 161-165
- • invasion of privacy, tort of, 164-165
- • • Canada historically not recognizing tort of invasion of privacy, 164
- • • law not settled in Ontario whether no tort of invasion of privacy, 164-165
- • • provincial privacy legislation establishing action for breach of privacy, 165
- • • Quebec's *Civil Code* establishing right to privacy, 165

Spyware and Malware — *cont'd*
• • • U.S. commentators indicating that tort could apply to spyware, 165
• • trespass to chattels, 161-164
• • • criticism in applying tort to protect new private property rights, 163-164
• • • direct interference with claimant's tangible personal property, 161
• • • spyware, 162-163
• • • technological protection measures (TPMs), non-consensual installation of, 163
• • • unauthorized robotic data collection ("web bots" or "spiders"), 162
• • • U.S. ISPs employing tort of trespass in targeting spam, 161-162
• *Competition Act*'s application to spyware, 157
• • deceptive marketing provisions, 157
• • misleading representations by spyware distributors, 157
• • remedies under Act, 157
• • "unfair and deceptive acts or practices" provisions in U.S., 157
• consumer awareness, 165-166
• • Anti-Spyware Coalition, 166
• • Canadian Internet Policy and Public Interest Clinic, 166
• • consumer activism, 166
• • Public Interest Advocacy Centre, 166
• *Criminal Code*'s application to malware and spyware, 151-155
• • generally, 155
• • • Canadian Task Force on Spam, 155
• • • practicality of enforcement being major problem, 155
• • mischief in relation to data, 154-155
• • • *Code* provision, 154
• • • malware producing prescribed effects, 154
• • • spyware interfering with user's enjoyment or operation, 154-155
• • unauthorized use of computer: s. 342.1, 151-154

• • • *Code* provision, 151-152
• • • "computer service" defined, 152
• • • fraud associated with malware or spyware, where, 153-154
• • • prosecution of authors and intentional distributors of malware, useful for, 152
• • • spyware intercepting computer functions and reporting back information, 153
• introduction, 149-151
• • "adware" applications, 150
• • distinction between malware and spyware, 149-150
• • invasive software triggering host of problems, 149
• • "malware", meaning of, 149
• • • Trojan horses, 149
• • spyware, categories of, 150
• • "spyware", meaning of, 149-151
• • • definition (FTC), 150-151
• • • form of data mining, 149
• • spyware, scope of, 151
• • technological pestilence, 149
• legislative reform, 158-161
• • Canadian Task Force on Spam recommendations re spam-related activities, 158
• • PIAC examining categories, risks and functions of spyware, 158
• • United States reform, 159-160
• • • CDT Report recommendations, 160
• • • FTC having concerns over legislative solutions, 160
• • • *Internet Spyware (I-SPY) Prevention Act of 2005*, 159
• • • *Securely Protect Yourself Against Cyber Trespass (Spy Act)*, 159-160
• *PIPEDA*'s application to spyware, 155-156
• • "commercial activities", 156
• • Federal Court proceedings being expensive and lengthy, 156
• • keystroke logging data constituting "personal information", 156, 156
• • spyware employed in commercial setting, 156

Template concordance with provincial legislation. *See also* **Internet Sales Contract Harmonization Template**
- additional exceptions, 58
- • Alberta, 58
- • Ontario, 58
- application of template, 55-56
- • Alberta, 55-56
- • British Columbia, 56
- • Manitoba, 56
- • Nova Scotia, 56
- • Ontario, 56
- • Template, 55
- cancellation of internet sales contract, 81-110
- • accept/decline not provided, express opportunity to, 83-84
- • • Alberta, 83
- • • British Columbia, 83
- • • Manitoba, 83
- • • Nova Scotia, 83
- • • Ontario, 84
- • • Template, 83
- • copy of contract not provided, 84
- • • Alberta, 84
- • • British Columbia, 84
- • • Manitoba, 84
- • • Nova Scotia, 84
- • • Ontario, 84
- • • Template, 84
- • court providing cancellation relief, 93-94
- • • Alberta, 93-94
- • • British Columbia, 94
- • • Manitoba, 94
- • • Nova Scotia, 94
- • • Ontario, 94
- • • Template, 93
- • deemed delivery of goods/ commencement of services, 89-93
- • • goods: delivery not possible, 90-91
- • • goods: delivery refused, 89-90
- • • services: commencement not possible, 92-93
- • • services: commencement refused, 91-92
- • delivery date or commencement date not specified, 87-89
- • • Alberta, 87
- • • British Columbia, 87-88
- • • Manitoba, 88-89
- • • Nova Scotia, 88
- • • Ontario, 88
- • • Template, 87
- • effect of cancellation, 99-101
- • • Alberta, 99
- • • British Columbia, 99-100
- • • Manitoba, 100
- • • Nova Scotia, 100
- • • Ontario, 100-101
- • failure to perform contract, 85-87
- • • Alberta, 85, 87
- • • British Columbia, 85-86
- • • Manitoba, 86
- • • Nova Scotia, 86-87
- • • Ontario, 86
- • • Template, 85
- • generally, 81-82
- • • Alberta, 81
- • • British Columbia, 82
- • • Manitoba, 82
- • • Nova Scotia, 82
- • • Ontario, 82
- • • Template, 81
- • notice of cancellation, 95-99
- • • form of notice, 96-98
- • • generally, 95-96
- • • notice deemed given when sent, 98-99
- • refund, recovery of, 109-110
- • • Alberta, 109
- • • British Columbia, 110
- • • Manitoba, 110
- • • Nova Scotia, 109
- • • Ontario, 110
- • • Template, 109
- • required information not provided, 82-83
- • • Alberta, 82
- • • British Columbia, 82
- • • Manitoba, 82
- • • Nova Scotia, 82
- • • Ontario, 83
- • • Template, 82

**Template concordance with
provincial legislation** — *cont'd*
- • responsibilities of consumer on
   cancellation, 102-108
- • • additional requirements, 108-109
- • • consumer required to return
   goods, 102-105
- • • goods deemed returned when
   sent, 106-108
- • responsibilities of seller on
   cancellation, 101-102, 105-108
- • • seller required to accept return,
   105-106
- • • seller required to pay reasonable
   shipping, 106
- • • seller required to refund, 101-102
- • supplier right of action, 109
- • • Alberta, 109
- • • British Columbia, 109
- • • Manitoba, 109
- • • Nova Scotia, 109
- • • Ontario, 109
- • • Template, 109
- • copy of internet sales contract, 74-81
- • information, required, 75-76
- • • Alberta, 75
- • • British Columbia, 75
- • • Manitoba, 75
- • • Nova Scotia, 75
- • • Ontario, 75-76
- • • Template, 75
- • seller to provide copy of agreement,
   74
- • • Alberta, 74
- • • British Columbia, 74
- • • Manitoba, 74
- • • Nova Scotia, 74
- • • Ontario, 74
- • • Template, 74
- • time and manner for providing
   copy, 76-81
- • • Alberta, 76-79
- • • British Columbia, 76-81
- • • Manitoba, 76-79
- • • Nova Scotia, 76-79
- • • Ontario, 76-79
- • • Template, 76-79
- • credit card charges, reversal of, 110-
   125

- • • charge, reversing, 117-118
- • • • Alberta, 117
- • • • British Columbia, 117
- • • • Manitoba, 117
- • • • Nova Scotia, 117-118
- • • • Ontario: discretionary reversal,
   118
- • • • Template, 117
- • • consumer able to request reversal,
   110-112
- • • • Alberta, 111
- • • • British Columbia, 111
- • • • Manitoba, 111
- • • • Nova Scotia, 111
- • • • Ontario, 111-112
- • • • Template, 110
- • • deemed given when sent, 119-120
- • • • additional requirements, 120
- • • • Alberta, 119
- • • • British Columbia, 119
- • • • Manitoba, 119
- • • • Nova Scotia, 119
- • • • Ontario, 119
- • • • Template, 119
- • • form of request, required, 112-113
- • • • Alberta, 112
- • • • British Columbia, 112
- • • • Manitoba, 112
- • • • Nova Scotia, 113
- • • • Ontario, 113
- • • • Template, 112
- • • information, required, 113-116
- • • • Alberta, 114
- • • • British Columbia, 114
- • • • Manitoba, 114-115
- • • • Nova Scotia, 115
- • • • Ontario, 115-116
- • • • Template, 113
- • • obligations of credit card issuer,
   116-117
- • • • Alberta, 116
- • • • British Columbia, 116
- • • • Manitoba, 116
- • • • Nova Scotia, 116
- • • • Ontario, 117
- • • • Template, 116
- • • method of request, 118-119
- • • • Alberta, 119
- • • • British Columbia, 119

Template concordance with provincial legislation — *cont'd*
- • • Manitoba, 119
- • • Nova Scotia, 119
- • • Ontario, 119
- • • Template, 118
- • offence, 120-122
- • • Alberta, 120-121
- • • British Columbia, 121
- • • Manitoba, 121
- • • Nova Scotia, 121
- • • Ontario, 121-122
- • • Template, 120
- • definitions, 46-55
- • • "consumer", 46-47
- • • Alberta, 46
- • • British Columbia, 46
- • • Manitoba, 47
- • • Nova Scotia, 47
- • • Ontario, 47
- • • Template, 46
- • • "consumer transaction", 47-48
- • • Alberta, 47
- • • British Columbia, 47-48
- • • Manitoba, 48
- • • Nova Scotia, 48
- • • Ontario, 47
- • • Template, 47
- • • "goods", 48-49
- • • Alberta, 48
- • • British Columbia, 49
- • • Manitoba, 49
- • • Nova Scotia, 49
- • • Ontario, 49
- • • Template, 48
- • • "internet", 49
- • • Alberta, 49
- • • British Columbia, 49
- • • Manitoba, 49
- • • Nova Scotia, 49
- • • Ontario, 49
- • • Template, 49
- • • "internet sales contract", 50
- • • Alberta, 50
- • • British Columbia, 50
- • • Manitoba, 50
- • • Nova Scotia, 50
- • • Ontario, 50
- • • Template, 50

- • • "services", 51-52
- • • Alberta, 51
- • • British Columbia, 51
- • • Manitoba, 51-52
- • • Nova Scotia, 52
- • • Ontario, 52
- • • Template, 51
- • • "supplier", 52-53
- • • Alberta, 52
- • • British Columbia, 52-53
- • • Manitoba, 53
- • • Nova Scotia, 53
- • • Ontario, 53
- • • Template, 52
- • variations, 53-55
- • • British Columbia, 53-54
- • • Manitoba, 54-55
- • disclosure of information, 58-73
- • clear and comprehensible, 71-72
- • • Alberta, 72
- • • British Columbia, 72
- • • Manitoba, 72
- • • Nova Scotia, 72
- • • Ontario, 72
- • • Template, 71
- • information accessed, 72
- • • Alberta, 72
- • • British Columbia, 72
- • • Manitoba, 72
- • • Nova Scotia, 72
- • • Ontario, 72
- • • Template, 72
- • information required in Template, 58-70
- • • accept/decline, express opportunity to, 70
- • • additional charges, 62-63
- • • additional provincial information requirements, 69-70
- • • cancellation, return, exchange and refund policies, 67-68
- • • currency for payment, 65
- • • date for delivery of goods or services beginning, 66
- • • delivery arrangements, 67
- • • description of goods or services, 61
- • • generally, 58-59

Template concordance with provincial legislation — *cont'd*
- • • payment, terms, conditions and method of, 65-66
- • • price of goods or services, 62
- • • restrictions, limitations or conditions, 68-69
- • • supplier's business address, 60
- • • supplier's name, 59
- • • supplier's telephone number, 60-61
- • • total amount of contract, 63-64
- • manner of disclosure, required, 71, 73
- • • Alberta, 71
- • • British Columbia, 71
- • • Manitoba, 71, 73
- • • Nova Scotia, 71
- • • Ontario, 71
- • • Template, 71
- • print, ability to, 73
- • • Alberta, 73
- • • British Columbia, 73
- • • Manitoba, 73
- • • Nova Scotia, 71
- • • Ontario, 73
- • • Template, 73
- • legislation, list of, 45-46
- • monetary limit, 56-57
- • Alberta, 56
- • British Columbia, 56-57
- • Manitoba, 57
- • Nova Scotia, 57
- • Ontario, 57
- • review/expiry, 123
- • Alberta, 123
- • waiver of rights not permitted, 122-123
- • Alberta, 122
- • British Columbia, 122
- • Manitoba, 122
- • Nova Scotia, 122
- • Ontario, 123

Trespass to chattels, 161-164. *See also* **Spyware and Malware**

Uniform Electronic Commerce Act (UECA). *See also* **Electronic contract**
- • application of Act, 9-10
- • carriage of goods, 17-18
- • • actions related to contracts of carriage of goods, 17-18
- • • document requirement, 18
- • communication of electronic documents, 15-17
- • • electronic agents, 15, 16
- • • • "electronic agent" defined, 15
- • • • involvement of, 16
- • • • material error when dealing with electronic agents, 16
- • • formation and operation of contracts, 15-16
- • • • offer or acceptance, 15-16
- • • sending and receipt of electronic documents, time and place of, 16-17
- • Crown, 1
- • definitions, 9
- • • "electronic", 9
- • • "electronic signature", 9
- • • "Government", 9
- • information, provision and retention of, 10-15
- • • collection, storage and transfer of documents or information, 15
- • • copies, 14
- • • legal recognition, 10
- • • non-electronic form satisfied by electronic document, 11-12
- • • original form, provision of, 12-13
- • • • integrity of information in electronic document, 12-13
- • • other requirements continuing to apply, 14
- • • payments, electronic, 15
- • • prescribed forms and manner of filing forms, 14
- • • retention of documents, 13-14
- • • • whether document capable of being retained, 13
- • • signatures, 12
- • • use not mandatory, 10-11
- • • writing requirement satisfied by electronic form, 11

0 1341 1381895 6

***Uniform Electronic Commerce Act
(UECA)*** — *cont'd*
- interpretation, 10
- introduction, 1-3
- • "click-wrap" contracts being
  enforceable in Canada, 2-3
- • • "clicking" designated icon on
    computer screen constituting offer
    or acceptance, 2
- • • electronic actions having legal
    contractual implications, 2-3
- • electronic agents resulting in
  binding contracts, interaction with,
  3
- • electronic equivalence of written
  and electronic communications, 1-2
- • rules governing formation of
  electronic contracts, 1-2
- • standards relating to contracting
  over open electronic networks, 1
- mailbox rule not stipulated under
  UECA, 4